ADVANCE PRAISE FOR ARTFUL MAKING

"Pay attention to what Austin and Devin are saying—their point of view represents an important expression of the new ethos of management."

—Dr. Eric Schmidt
Chairman and CEO, Google

"Austin and Devin's *Artful Making* provides profound new insight on one of the most critical issues in business today—routinely achieving great results from knowledge-based workers. Their rich commentary articulates a groundbreaking framework and blueprint for more effective management."

—Joe Liemandt
Founder and CEO, Trilogy

"Austin and Devin have written a useful field guide to the art—and science—of managing complexity, full of clues on how to wrestle with the uncertainties of leading a successful 21st century enterprise."

—Tom Kelley
General Manager, IDEO, author of The Art of
Innovation

"No book in the past decade has influenced me as profoundly as *Artful Making*. The authors' genius is in contrasting the delivery of a theatrical production with the design of systems and discovering the processes are virtually identical, that current best practices in each can inform and improve the results in the other."

—F. Warren McFarlan
*Albert H. Gordon Professor of Business
Administration, Harvard Business School*

"Great companies and managers of the 21st century will emerge because they embrace the concepts in this book. Those who learn to adapt to ambiguity, attract deep thinkers and yet remain passionate and focused on practical solutions will win."

—Roy Singham
CEO and President, ThoughtWorks

"Mindbending! I will be giving a copy to every manager of teams I coach."

—Kent Beck
Author of Extreme Programming: Embrace Change

"Knowledge work is inherently different from production work. Austin and Devin have written the definitive statement on that difference, and the definitive statement on managing knowledge workers."

—Tom DeMarco
Author of Peopleware (*with Tim Lister*) *and* Slack:
Getting Past Burnout, Busywork, and the Myth of
Total Efficiency

"I applaud Rob Austin and Lee Devin's creative work shown clearly in *Artful Making*. It gives us an insightful and revolutionary approach to how we create and innovate. They have captured the essential qualities and key factors that lead to successfully leading knowledge-based work teams. We have been working in knowledge-based teams for many years without much understanding of how best to harness the potential. *Artful Making* gives us new insights and a new perspective that truly challenge the conventional approach to creating new products and services."

—Christine Davis
Visiting Scientist, Carnegie Mellon University, former EVP and General Manager, Raytheon

"*Artful Making* introduces a completely novel and very practical way to think about managing software processes. Parallels to the theatre ring entirely true, and Austin and Devin's analyses make the parallels useful."

—Lucinda Duncalfe Holt
Financial services industry consultant and former software company CEO

"In *Artful Making*, Austin and Devin forge a unique partnership of IT expert and play-maker, providing a lens for the reader to see processes required for creation of knowledge assets. The power of their lens helps to clear the fog surrounding many heretofore hazy ideas and concepts. The reader sees that "products" in this new century are not finite, physical things, but are bundles of customer-defined value possessing an overall consistency, made dynamically by teams of knowledge workers. The "how" these knowledge-based "products" are made is revealed by the wonderful insights in this must-read book for today's manager."

—Richard L. Nolan
William Barclay Harding Professor of Business Administration, Harvard Business School

"In *Artful Making*, Rob Austin and Lee Devin challenge us to acknowledge the new world we live and work in. *Artful Making* is peppered with insightful stories from such odd bedfellows as the artistic world of theatre, pre-industrial medieval guilds, and today's knowledge-based corporations. The qualities of artful making direct us to reconceive our view of management, development efforts, and teams for profound impact. The insights found within these pages lead one to reflect on changes we should make to all of our creative endeavors."

—Skip Shuda
Chief Technology Officer, Calder Systems, Entrepreneur, founder of Destiny WebSolutions

"... underlying structural similarities in costs make theatre rehearsal and other collaborative art processes better models for much knowledge work than more rules-based, scientific processes." Thus begins Professors Austin and Devin's fascinating account of *Artful Making*. Acknowledging that, in the 21st century, clear objectives and processes are a luxury that often can't be afforded, the authors masterfully demonstrate how practices followed in the collaborative arts and theatre in particular offer a model and a process for management. In a media world challenged by rapid technology changes, increased distribution channels, and volatile market conditions, *Artful Making* offers a clear roadmap for success.

—José Royo
Vice President, New Products, Ascent Media Group

ARTFUL MAKING

ISBN 0-13-008695-9

In an increasingly competitive world, it is quality
of thinking that gives an edge, an idea that opens new
doors, a technique that solves a problem, or an insight
that simply helps make sense of it all.

We work with leading authors in the various arenas
of business and finance to bring cutting-edge thinking
and best learning practice to a global market.

It is our goal to create world-class print publications
and electronic products that give readers
knowledge and understanding they can
apply while studying or at work.

To find out more about our business
products, you can visit us at www.ft-ph.com

ARTFUL MAKING

What Managers
Need to Know About
How Artists Work

ROB AUSTIN · LEE DEVIN

Foreword by Dr. Eric Schmidt, Chairman and CEO, Google

FT Prentice Hall

FINANCIAL TIMES

An Imprint of PEARSON EDUCATION
Upper Saddle River, NJ • New York • San Francisco • Toronto • Sydney
Tokyo • Singapore • Hong Kong • Cape Town • Madrid
Paris • Milan • Munich • Amsterdam

www.ft-ph.com

A Cataloging-in-Publication Data record for this book
can be obtained from the Library of Congress.

Editorial/Production Supervision: *Wil Mara*
Executive Editor: *Tim Moore*
Editorial Assistant: *Richard Winkler*
Marketing Manager: *John Pierce*
Manufacturing Buyer: *Maura Zaldivar*
Cover Design Director: *Jerry Votta*
Cover Designer: *Anthony Gemmellaro*
Composition: *Daly Graphics*

 ©2003 by Pearson Education, Inc.
Publishing as Financial Times Prentice Hall
Upper Saddle River, New Jersey 07458

Financial Times Prentice Hall books are widely used by corporations and
government agencies for training, marketing, and resale.

Financial Times Prentice Hall offers excellent discounts on this book when ordered in
quantity for bulk purchases or special sales. For more information, please contact:
U.S. Corporate and Government Sales, 1-800-382-3419, corpsales@pearsontech-
group.com. For sales outside of the U.S., please contact: International Sales, 1-317-
581-3793, international@pearsontechgroup.com.

Company and product names mentioned herein are the trademarks
or registered trademarks of their respective owners.

Printed in the United States of America

First Printing

ISBN 0-13-008695-9

Pearson Education Ltd.
Pearson Education Australia Pty., Ltd.
Pearson Education Singapore, Pte. Ltd.
Pearson Education North Asia, Ltd.
Pearson Education Canada, Ltd.
Pearson Educación de Mexico, S.A. de C.V.
Pearson Education—Japan
Pearson Education Malaysia, Pte. Ltd.

FINANCIAL TIMES PRENTICE HALL BOOKS

For more information, please go to www.ft-ph.com

Business and Technology
Sarv Devaraj and Rajiv Kohli
   The IT Payoff: Measuring the Business Value of Information Technology Investments
Nicholas D. Evans
   Business Agility: Strategies for Gaining Competitive Advantage through Mobile Business Solutions
Nicholas D. Evans
   Business Innovation and Disruptive Technology: Harnessing the Power of Breakthrough Technology…for Competitive Advantage
Nicholas D. Evans
   Consumer Gadgets: 50 Ways to Have Fun and Simplify Your Life with Today's Technology…and Tomorrow's
Faisal Hoque
   The Alignment Effect: How to Get Real Business Value Out of Technology
Thomas Kern, Mary Cecelia Lacity, and Leslie P. Willcocks
   Netsourcing: Renting Business Applications and Services Over a Network

Ecommerce
Dale Neef
   E-procurement: From Strategy to Implementation

Economics
David Dranove
   What's Your Life Worth? Health Care Rationing…Who Lives? Who Dies? Who Decides?
David R. Henderson
   The Joy of Freedom: An Economist's Odyssey
Jonathan Wight
   Saving Adam Smith: A Tale of Wealth, Transformation, and Virtue

Entrepreneurship
Oren Fuerst and Uri Geiger
   From Concept to Wall Street
David Gladstone and Laura Gladstone
   Venture Capital Handbook: An Entrepreneur's Guide to Raising Venture Capital, Revised and Updated
Erica Orloff and Kathy Levinson, Ph.D.
   The 60-Second Commute: A Guide to Your 24/7 Home Office Life
Jeff Saperstein and Daniel Rouach
   Creating Regional Wealth in the Innovation Economy: Models, Perspectives, and Best Practices

Finance

Aswath Damodaran
The Dark Side of Valuation: Valuing Old Tech, New Tech, and New Economy Companies

Kenneth R. Ferris and Barbara S. Pécherot Petitt
Valuation: Avoiding the Winner's Curse

International Business

Fernando Robles, Françoise Simon, and Jerry Haar
Winning Strategies for the New Latin Markets

Investments

Harry Domash
Fire Your Stock Analyst! Analyzing Stocks on Your Own

Philip Jenks and Stephen Eckett, Editors
The Global-Investor Book of Investing Rules: Invaluable Advice from 150 Master Investors

Charles P. Jones
Mutual Funds: Your Money, Your Choice. Take Control Now and Build Wealth Wisely

D. Quinn Mills
Buy, Lie, and Sell High: How Investors Lost Out on Enron and the Internet Bubble

John Nofsinger and Kenneth Kim
Infectious Greed: Restoring Confidence in America's Companies

John R. Nofsinger
Investment Blunders (of the Rich and Famous)...And What You Can Learn from Them

John R. Nofsinger
Investment Madness: How Psychology Affects Your Investing...And What to Do About It

Leadership

Jim Despain and Jane Bodman Converse
And Dignity for All: Unlocking Greatness through Values-Based Leadership

Marshall Goldsmith, Vijay Govindarajan, Beverly Kaye, and Albert A. Vicere
The Many Facets of Leadership

Frederick C. Militello, Jr., and Michael D. Schwalberg
Leverage Competencies: What Financial Executives Need to Lead

Eric G. Stephan and Wayne R. Pace
Powerful Leadership: How to Unleash the Potential in Others and Simplify Your Own Life

Management

Marketing

Michael Basch
CustomerCulture: How FedEx and Other Great Companies Put the Customer First Every Day

Deirdre Breakenridge
Cyberbranding: Brand Building in the Digital Economy

Jonathan Cagan and Craig M. Vogel
Creating Breakthrough Products: Innovation from Product Planning to Program Approval

James W. Cortada
21st Century Business: Managing and Working in the New Digital Economy

Al Lieberman, with Patricia Esgate
The Entertainment Marketing Revolution: Bringing the Moguls, the Media, and the Magic to the World

Tom Osenton
Customer Share Marketing: How the World's Great Marketers Unlock Profits from Customer Loyalty

Yoram J. Wind and Vijay Mahajan, with Robert Gunther
Convergence Marketing: Strategies for Reaching the New Hybrid Consumer

Public Relations

Gerald R. Baron
Now Is Too Late: Survival in an Era of Instant News

Deirdre Breakenridge and Thomas J. DeLoughry
The New PR Toolkit: Strategies for Successful Media Relations

Strategy

Thomas L. Barton, William G. Shenkir, and Paul L. Walker
Making Enterprise Risk Management Pay Off: How Leading Companies Implement Risk Management

Henry A. Davis and William W. Sihler
Financial Turnarounds: Preserving Enterprise Value

CONTENTS

CHAPTER 5   ARTFUL MAKING AS PART OF THE SHIFT TO A KNOWLEDGE ECONOMY   57

The most remarkable technological innovations occur when small teams of people are free to explore the outer limits of their imaginations. In my 20-plus years of experience in the fast-moving high-tech industry at Sun, Novell, and now Google, few facts have seemed as consistently clear as this one.

You can see this in how the best companies do R&D. They do it bottom up, not top down. Microsoft® is a great example of this. Observers are often surprised by how much autonomy the various groups at Microsoft have. It's very much a bottom-up culture. All of the successful high tech companies have had to adopt this model except the chip companies. They're different because chips have really long lead times, are so complicated, and require so many people. (In Austin and Devin's terms, they have industrial making characteristics.) But for much else in the tech industry, especially software, it's possible and desirable to be decentralized. You need to let the artists explore and create the next great thing, which they will do reliably if you permit it.

In *Artful Making: What Managers Need to Know About How Artists Work*, Rob Austin and Lee Devin provide a long-awaited and extremely important way of thinking about how to manage the artful aspects of business. All of us who manage talented, idiosyncratic people know there's art involved. We routinely support exploration for which we, as managers, don't immediately see the point because—as Austin and Devin point out—great ideas often *emerge*. You can't get to them by taking the most direct route because you don't know the destination in advance. You think you're working on one thing, but the really important thing turns out to be something else entirely, something on the periphery of what you thought was important. I've seen this happen again and again.

For example, Java™ was originally thought of as a technology with relatively limited scope, useful in TV set-top boxes, that sort of thing. The story related in the first chapter of this book demonstrates how we, at Sun, came around to the realization that the Internet and Java combined in a way that would create a tectonic shift in the technology landscape, one that could greatly benefit the company's bottom line. The same thing was true at Novell with our innovative ZENworks product. We originally thought the ZENworks project was about one thing but it turned out to be about something much different, and much more important.

When I arrived at Google, I discovered that the founders, Sergey (Brin) and Larry (Page), had a great appreciation for letting the artists work (and play), and for the emergent character of important innovations. They had established the kind of management style and culture at Google that nurtures artful exploration and innovation, and I'm doing my best to keep that alive.

As Austin and Devin also point out, the management methods you use when you rely on emergent innovations can seem pretty foreign to people who have been steeped in the methods of industrial-age companies. But in the high-tech world (and probably in many other industries), being able to manage creative engineers so that they will produce emergent innovations is absolutely crucial. This is partially because the environment is changing so fast that it requires improvisation in terms of strategy, products, and even day-to-day operations. Just when you think you understand the technology landscape, you see a major disruption.

The reason high tech is so hard to follow is that disruptions come without warning. Just like our major innovations, disruptions come from the corner of your business model where you're not expecting them. In fact, one company's innovation is another's disruption. Java was an innovation for Sun but a disruption for its competitors. How you prepare yourself for unexpected shifts will determine how you'll do in the long run in high-tech or any business where uncertainty reigns. In my opinion, this will be increasingly true in many less knowledge-work-oriented industries. As information and telecommunications technologies create new possibilities for tectonic shifts in those businesses, the messages in this book will become increasingly vital.

At Google we use many of the techniques described in *Artful Making*, though we don't necessarily call them the same things. For example, we often organize our people into what we call "Googlets," which are much like what Austin and Devin call "Ensembles"—teams of three or four engineers who are sent on missions of exploration and innovation. What Googlets come back with is often unexpected, but just as often exciting and profitable.

There's little doubt in my mind that our Googlets are engaged in collaborative art. I've sometimes argued that, in fact, it goes beyond art—that it's nothing short of magic. Austin and Devin demystify the magic and give us terrific insights into how it is made. In the process, they debunk the myth that this magic is unreliable. It's not. It has a structure. It is rigorous. And it *is* reliable—as long as you furnish an environment in which your people can do it and keep creating it.

Austin and Devin also place their ideas in a very important historical context. They show how value creation in the information age will increasingly rely on figuring out how to get the most out of your people. They also suggest that this shift in the way we work is every bit as important as the shift precipitated by the industrial revolution. What is perhaps most exciting to me about this suggestion is that it implies, as I believe, that human values ultimately win out over mechanistic values or technology for its own sake in an increasingly technological world. Companies, especially high-techs, are not machines. They are collections of tremendously motivated and creative people, and it is their intrinsic motivation and their creativity that makes all the difference.

Pay attention to what Austin and Devin are saying—their point of view represents an important expression of the new ethos of management. If you frequently find yourself trying to steer your organization without a clear idea of where you'll end up, and improvising mid-course corrections in response to emergent problems, then this book is for you.

Dr. Eric Schmidt
Chairman and CEO, Google
January 2003
Mountain View, California

MANAGING WHEN YOU DON'T
KNOW WHERE YOU'RE GOING

If you don't know where you're going, any map will do.[1] This conventional wisdom sounds right to many managers. It highlights the safety of having a clear objective for your management actions. It implies that all management actions are likely to be confused and inefficient if you don't have a clear objective. If you don't have a good fix on your destination—be it a product or service, a strategic or competitive outcome, or anything else—you may as well not start the journey.

For a lot of your work, though, this so-called wisdom is wrong. Why? For one thing, you can't always know your destination in advance. Whether you're designing a new product, running a business in volatile conditions, operating a process that might encounter unforeseen inputs, or just trying to figure out what to do with your life, the journey usually involves exploration, adjustment, and improvisation. Situations in which you don't or can't know the results in advance are common and consequential. All businesses face them.

If you're not too narrow in what you're willing to call "management," you can manage these situations. You can enhance effectiveness and efficiency, and you can improve the likelihood of valuable outcomes. However, the methods you'll use will differ from, and sometimes conflict with, methods that work when you do know where you're going.

There is an increasingly important category of work—knowledge work—that you can best manage by not enforcing a detailed, in-advance set of objectives, even if you could. Often in this kind of work, time spent planning what you want to do will be better spent actually doing (or letting others in your charge do), trying something you haven't thought out in detail so you can quickly incorporate what you learn from the experience in the next attempt. In appropriate conditions—only in appropriate conditions—you can gain more value from experience than from up-front analysis. In certain kinds of work, even if you can figure out where you're going and find a map to get you there, that may not be the best thing to do.

Forging ahead without detailed specifications to guide you obviously requires innovation, new actions. We take this observation one step further by suggesting that knowledge work, which adds value in large part because of its capacity for innovation, can and often should be structured as artists structure their work. Managers should look to collaborative artists rather than to more traditional management models if they want to create economic value in this new century.

> In knowledge work, often you can best manage by not enforcing a detailed, in-advance set of objectives, even when you could. Time spent planning what you want to do will be better spent actually doing, trying something you haven't thought out in detail, so you can quickly incorporate what you learn from the experience in the next attempt.

We call this approach *artful making*. "Artful," because it derives from the theory and practice of collaborative art and requires an artist-like attitude from managers and team members. "Making," because it requires that you conceive of your work as altering or combining materials into a form, for a purpose.[2] Materials thus treated become something new, something they would not become without the intervention of a maker. This definition usually points to work that changes physical materials, iron ore and charcoal into steel, for instance. But the work and management we're considering don't always do that. Instead they mostly operate in imagination, in the realm of knowledge and ideas. While artful making improves any thing that exhibits interdependency among its parts, we're not primarily concerned with heating metal and beating it into shapes. We're more concerned with strategies, product designs, or software—new things that groups create by thinking, talking, and collaborating.

ARTFUL MAKING

Any activity that involves creating something entirely new requires artful making. Whenever you have no blueprint to tell you in detail what to do, you must work artfully. A successful response to an unexpected move by a competitor requires artful activity; so does handling a sudden problem caused by a supplier. An artful manager operates without the safety net of a detailed specification, guiding a team or organization when no one knows exactly where it's going.

In the 21st Century, it's a simple fact that you often don't know where you're going when you start a journey. A manager who needs to be handed a clear set of objectives or a process specification is only half a manager (and not the most important half). To know where you're going by the time you start, that's an amazing luxury and you probably can't afford it. Anyway, if you think you know where you're going, you're probably wrong. The need to innovate, to make midcourse corrections, and to adapt to changing conditions are the main features of a growing part of daily work.

Many people in business admit that parts of their work are "more art than science." What they often mean, alas, is that they don't understand those parts. "Art" used in a business context usually refers to something done by "talented" or "creative" people who are not quite trustworthy, who do work that resists reasonable description. There's often a disparaging implication that art-like processes are immature, that they have not yet evolved to incorporate the obviously superior methods of science. The premise that underlies this point of view equates progress with the development of reliable, rules-based procedures to replace flaky, unreliable, art-based processes. We reject this premise.

> A theatre company consistently delivers a valuable, innovative product under the pressure of a very firm deadline (opening night). The product, a play, executes with great precision, incorporating significant innovations every time, but finishing within 30 seconds of the same length every time.

Our close examination of art-based processes shows that they're understandable and reliable, capable of sophisticated innovation at levels many "scientific" business processes can't achieve. A theatre company, for instance, consistently delivers a valuable, innovative product under the pressure of a very firm deadline (opening night, eight o'clock curtain). The product, a play, executes again and again with great precision, incorporating significant innovations every time, but finishing within 30 seconds of the same length every time. And although art-based processes realize the full capabilities of talented workers and can benefit from great worker talent, by no means do they require exceptional or especially creative individuals. Nor does great individual talent ensure a valuable outcome. A company of exceptionally talented big stars can (and often will) create a less effective play than one made up of ordinarily talented artists who have, through hard work, learned how to collaborate. Business history too provides numerous examples of underdog upstarts out-collaborating and out-executing companies with much better resources; and few (if any) companies have ever worshiped more devoutly at the altar of raw individual talent than Enron, one of the most spectacular corporate failures in history.[3]

As we will show, underlying structural similarities in costs make theatre rehearsal and other collaborative art processes better models for knowledge work than more rules-based, scientific processes. The key to understanding these similarities is something we call *cheap and rapid iteration*.

How Cheap and Rapid Iteration Changes Everything

The *cost of iteration*—the cost of reconfiguring a process and then running it again—significantly impacts the way we work. Reconfiguring an auto assembly process can involve buying and installing new equipment, which can be pretty expensive. So, automakers usually do a lot of planning before they commit to a configuration. They don't want to have to reconfigure very often. They try to "Get it right the first time."

On the other hand, some software development processes are designed nowadays so that they can be reconfigured cheaply and quickly. Developers generate new versions of a software system as often as needed. Technologies that allow new versions to be rebuilt easily keep the cost of iteration low. When enabling technologies help keep the cost of iteration low, we don't need to worry as much about getting it right the first time. Instead, we can try things, learn from them, then reconfigure and try again. Because it doesn't cost much to iterate, the value of doing is greater than the value of thinking about how to do. Cheap and rapid iteration allows us to substitute experience for planning. Rather than "Get it right the first time," our battle cry becomes "Make it great before the deadline."

Management researchers often talk about cheap and rapid iteration as cheap and rapid *experimentation*. The ability to run experiments cheaply and quickly is an important benefit when the cost of iteration is low. Simulation technologies, for example, allow automakers to run virtual crash-testing experiments to determine the safety implications of many car body structures, more than they could afford to test with actual cars.[4] But experimentation, though important, is only part of what is achieved by cheap and rapid iteration. If you think and talk about iteration as experimentation, low cost of iteration seems to make business more like science. Its broader effect, though, is to make business more like art.

Cheap and rapid iteration allows us to substitute experience for planning. Rather than "Get it right the first time," our battle cry becomes "Make it great before the deadline."

Here's why: Before you can crash test virtual cars, you must create virtual cars. Cheap and rapid iteration lets you test cars more cheaply, but it also lets you create them more cheaply, and in many more forms. The creation of things to test—in scientific terms, the generation of hypotheses—is a fundamentally creative act. In many business situations, the hypothesis, problem, or opportunity is not well-defined, nor does it present itself tidily formed; you must therefore create it. Even when a problem or opportunity appears well-defined, often you can benefit from conceiving it in a new form. The form you conceive for it—the idea of it you have—will determine how (and how well) you solve it. Cheap and rapid experimentation lets you try new forms; cheap and rapid artful iteration helps you create new forms to try.

Artful making (which includes agile software development, theatre rehearsal, some business strategy creation, and much of other knowledge work) is a process for creating form out of disorganized materials. Collaborating artists, using the human brain as their principal technology and ideas as their principal material, work with a very low cost of iteration. They try something and then try it again a different way, constantly reconceiving ambiguous circumstances and variable materials into coherent and valuable outputs.

Artful making differs from what we call *industrial making*, which emphasizes the importance of detailed planning, as well as tightly specified objectives, processes, and products. Its principles are familiar: Pull apart planning and production to specialize each; create a blueprint or specification, then conform to it; don't do anything before you know you can do everything; "Get it right the first time." When industrial makers conform to plans and specifications, they say their products and processes have "quality." The principles of industrial making are so embedded in business thinking that they're transparent and we don't notice them. We apply them reflexively; they are "The way we do things." But, as we shall see, industrial methods can distort reality and smother innovation. Artful and industrial making are distinct approaches and each must be applied in the appropriate conditions.

It's important to recognize that artful and industrial making are not mutually exclusive. Artful making doesn't replace industrial making. Artful making should not be applied everywhere, nor should industrial making. They complement each other and often can be used in combination. Complementary doesn't mean interchangeable, though. As opportunities for artful making multiply with the expansion of the knowledge work sector of business, managers and other workers must be careful not to attempt to solve artistic problems with industrial methods, and vice versa.

THE HISTORY AND ORIGINS OF THIS BOOK

The collaboration that led to this book began with a telephone call in 1998. Rob (a business professor) asked Lee (a theatre professor) to repeat a story he'd told when Rob was his student at Swarthmore in the early 1980s. The story was about different ways of controlling human action. When he called,

Rob was trying to understand why control mechanisms that work well for physical activities seem to work less well for knowledge work. Lee recognized some of the issues from conversations with his son, Sean (then an engineer/manager at Allied Signal); they had been casually wondering how to apply principles of theatre improvisation to the reluctance of engineers to look beyond the back of the book for solutions to new problems. A subsequent series of increasingly energetic conversations between Rob and Lee turned to broader issues of how highly skilled people engaged in creative activities might be managed (or "directed," as Lee put it).

If you think and talk about iteration as experimentation, low cost of iteration seems to make business more like science. Its broader effect, though, is to make business more like art.

We were surprised to discover common patterns and structures in our separate domains. Rob talked about software development; Lee talked about play making. But the issues sounded oddly, and increasingly, similar. Some recent ideas and methods in software development, especially in the so-called "agile" community, seemed almost identical to theatre methods. As this became more obvious, an idea dawned on business professor Rob: *These artists are much better at this than we are.* Managers and management students don't understand how to create on cue, how to innovate reliably on a deadline, something theatre companies do all the time.

We quickly noticed something else. As Rob tried to understand how theatre ensembles innovate in rehearsal, he kept missing the point; or so it seemed to Lee. Now, missing the point isn't an entirely new experience for Rob, but there was more to this problem than intellectual density. As Rob listened and tried to repeat back what he heard, Lee and the artists at the People's Light and Theatre Company gradually took on an aspect of polite rather than interested attention. Eyes glazed and conversation grew desultory. Rob's management language didn't accommodate the theatre's idea of work. An example will help illustrate what we mean.

Early in this research, thinking about cheap and rapid iteration as a way of working, we found ourselves talking about "failure." Rob observed that an iterative work cycle must include many failures on the way to success. Lee agreed, but resisted the term "failure." Failure isn't the right idea. In rehearsal, the iterations all interact with each other. The current run-through provides the main material for the next run-through. Each trial is a necessary step on the way to what's good and essential to the final success. To call an essential step toward success a failure merely tortures language. What's more, the word "failure" applied to routine work could poison the growth of Ensemble, a quality of group work essential to rehearsal, and to artful making. "Fair enough," thought Rob, "use some other word," though it seemed at the time like a minor technical point.

Then we got to thinking about IDEO, a leading product design firm that employs an iterative approach, and failure came up again.[5] We agreed that IDEO's work process was an artful one, but they talk about failure all the time, saying things like, "Fail often to succeed sooner." When professors at the Harvard Business School (HBS) use IDEO as an example, it's customary to note the difference between a "failure" and a "mistake." In the HBS view, IDEO cherishes failure because it generates new information. But a failure that doesn't generate useful new information is called a mistake. Touch a hot stove and burn your hand—that's a failure; touch it again and burn your hand again—that's a mistake—same injury, no new information.

This resonates with many Master of Business Administration (MBA) students and even executives, but makes no sense to artists. The distinction between failure and mistake imposes an unreasonable limit on exploration. Though artful making is, as we have said, reliable and efficient, it has little use for the efficiency of rules like "Avoid touching a hot stove twice." Touching the stove twice (or ten times) may be what's needed to break up a creative log jam. Just as an athlete may need to execute the same painful movements (lift the weight; run the interval) over and over on the way to new levels of performance, so you may need to make the same mistake many times on the way to an innovative leap. Burning your hand is a small price to pay for a good idea.

We concluded from these discussions that we had to be careful about the fit between artful making ideas and management thinking categories. Describing theatre practice in Rob's vocabulary, we risked missing the point.

In the 21st Century, a manager who needs to be handed a clear objective or process specification to be effective is only half a manager (and not the most important half).

How to Read This Book

For the above reasons, we resolved in our study to describe and understand theatre in some detail as a way to describe and understand a big change in the way we think about work. We'll rely on the persuasive power of an extended analogy to combine with your experience and spark new ways of thinking. Very little of what we discuss in this book is substantively new. Iterative product development processes, for instance, are well-documented in management literature. What's new here isn't the raw content, but the suggestion to use theatre art as a lens that can offer a new and productive view of familiar, but rapidly changing territory.

In the chapters that follow, we will provide evidence of our claim that some successful business processes are becoming more and more like art. We will also describe in detail the artful making framework, an enabling metaphor to replace more traditional industrial metaphors that control how we manage and do work. Early chapters will focus on explaining what we mean by artful making, and how it manifests in many different environments. Later chapters will illustrate how companies, both business and theatre, make artfully. In doing all this, we will sometimes take you quite deeply into the inner workings of artists in a theatre ensemble. As you read the "artsy" sections of this book, we encourage you to consider our extended analogy between theatre and business with an open mind. The analogy is not a perfect map in all respects, but it may contain useful insights, including some particular to your unique situation, unknown to us, that you must therefore discover for yourself.

ENDNOTES

1. *ALICE:* Would you tell me, please, which way I ought to go from here?

   CHESHIRE CAT: That depends a good deal on where you want to get to.

   ALICE: I don't much care where—

   CHESHIRE CAT: Then it doesn't matter which way you go.

   ALICE:—as long as I get somewhere.

   CHESHIRE CAT: Oh, you're sure to do that, if only you walk long enough.

   Lewis Carroll, *Alice's Adventures in Wonderland; Through the Looking Glass* (New York: Collier Books, 1962) p. 82.

2. This formulation was conceived first by Aristotle about 2500 years ago. He applied it to unique products composed of interdependent parts: handmade, unique things, in other words. This way of looking at making fell out of favor as making more and more referred to vast numbers of things mass-produced.

3. See, for example, Malcolm Gladwell, "The Talent Myth," *The New Yorker* (July 22, 2002) pp. 26–33.

4. Michael Schrage has written about how simulation helps companies behave in ways that we would call artful. *Serious Play: How the World's Best Companies Simulate to Innovate* (Boston: Harvard Business School Press, 2000).

5. For more information on IDEO, see Tom Kelley's *The Art of Innovation: Lessons in Creativity from IDEO, America's Leading Design Firm* (New York: Random House, 2001). Or, for a shorter summary, see Stefan Thomke and Ashok Nimgade, "IDEO Product Development" (Harvard Business School case no. 600-143, 2000).

1 WHAT'S REALLY DIFFERENT ABOUT KNOWLEDGE WORK

Just about everybody recognizes that work is changing as we enter the 21st Century. When we refer to this change, we talk about a shift from an industrial economy to an information economy, from physical work to knowledge work. But we don't yet really know how to think about the evolving nature of work. We still base our frameworks and metaphors solidly on learning from the previous era. We know our industrial age thought patterns intimately. We're comfortable with them. We love them because they are so successful for us as we strive to work and manage well, to create economic value, wealth, and improved standards of living.

It would be convenient if our accumulated industrial era understanding extended perfectly into the information age, if the future of management projected smoothly from its past. But it doesn't. The sooner we admit this and get on with the task of new learning, the sooner we'll be able to push on to even greater economic success.

Let's be clear about what we are claiming: As business becomes more dependent on knowledge to create value, work becomes more like art. In the future, managers who understand how artists work will have an advantage over those who don't.

This book proposes a framework, an "enabling metaphor," for doing and managing knowledge work. We draw this framework from a source that may seem strange at first, the collaborative arts. This is no cute spin or angle. Let's be clear about what we are claiming: As business becomes more dependent on knowledge to create value, *work becomes more like art*. In the future, managers who understand how artists work will have an advantage over those who don't. The implications of business becoming more "art-like" must be taken into account as we seek to manage knowledge work and knowledge workers. Management methods born in the factory or descended from industrial age ideas don't successfully manage artists making a play, and they don't successfully manage cutting-edge software developers. People use terms like "software engineering," "knowledge management systems," and "product development factories," unaware that these industrial metaphors, once so enabling, have become restrictive. When your product is "thoughtstuff,"[1] imagining your methods in factory terms holds back your originality. At a certain level of routine, these metaphors still function effectively, but leaders in an increasingly wide range of knowledge work need to move on. That's where this book comes in.

We'll show that successful methods now evolving in business increasingly resemble those of artists, that management of modern knowledge work resembles directing a theatre ensemble more than it resembles supervising a factory floor. And, given this, we'll suggest a new enabling metaphor as a tool for thinking about work and management, illustrating it with art and business examples.

We badly need this alternative metaphor. Without it, our industrial age reflexes cause us to fall back on industrial metaphors. Deep in our hearts, we all know the factory is the wrong model for knowledge work. As friend and colleague Tom DeMarco has aptly put it, the factory metaphor is "the elephant in the bathtub that all us other bathers are pretending not to notice."[2] Even people who admit the different nature of knowledge work have difficulty accepting the full implications of the differences. That elephant is troublesome, we concede, but we cling to its attractive qualities.

Let's be equally clear about what we are *not* saying here. We are *not* advocating "loose" management. The idea that arts practice is less rigorous than business practice is a major misconception. We're not proposing that you give up structure or discipline or fiscal responsibility. We *are* proposing alternate ways to achieve them. If you think arts practitioners are somehow less constrained, that they "have it easier" than businesspeople, you are incorrect.[3]

In the multi-year study that supports this book, we identified striking structural similarities between artists' methods and methods that have recently appeared in some business areas. We became convinced that theatre practice, agile software development, some new methods of strategy making and project management, and activities in many other business areas are examples of a more general phenomenon we call *artful making*. This book describes how artful makers (executives, managers, and team members) respond to challenges increasingly prevalent in business environments, how their responses differ from those of "industrial makers." We begin our story with three real-life illustrations of what we mean by artful and industrial making in business and in art.

> The idea that arts practice is less rigorous than business practice is a major misconception. If you think arts practitioners are somehow less constrained, that they "have it easier" than businesspeople, you are incorrect.

ARTFUL AND INDUSTRIAL MAKING IN ACTION

Real work almost always includes elements of both artful and industrial making, sometimes in appropriate combination, other times not (in which case, disappointing outcomes generally result). Some situations call primarily for artful making, others primarily for industrial making. As Sun Microsystems came to embrace Web technologies, their approach was, as we shall see, mostly artful. At Ford Motor Company, the approach was discernibly different, mostly industrial. Both firms successfully adopted the new technologies. Neither provides a perfect example of an artful or industrial approach.[4] Even so, comparing these stories with each other, and then with a rehearsal at the People's Light and Theatre Company, will begin to explain the differences between artful and industrial ways of working and managing.

REALIZING THE IMPORTANCE OF WEB TECHNOLOGIES AT SUN MICROSYSTEMS[5]

Sun's use of the Web began in early 1993, when a curious Sun engineer downloaded an early Web browser that had just been made available for public distribution. The engineer began tinkering with the new technology, setting up his own workstation as a Web server. He showed it to other engineers, who also began playing with it. This handful of experimenters set up easy ways for others to install Web servers and browsers on their workstations. The technology spread like wildfire throughout the firm. Someone showed it to Sun's engineering vice president, who found it interesting enough to support the creation of an external Web site, but this didn't command much attention from other senior managers. No formal initiative supported the site or acknowledged the developing grassroots interest.

The Web got management's attention in March 1994, when Web traffic on the company's network caused an entire plant to shut down by blocking customer orders. Most of Sun's senior managers first met the Web in this unfortunate context: Unauthorized employee activity had created a serious business problem. Some managers wanted to disallow employee use of the Web, but cooler heads prevailed. Sun maintained an employee culture that encouraged exploration; a blanket order prohibiting Web use would have an unhealthy effect on that culture and would not go over well with employees.

Networking engineers knew how to solve the problem, but they needed time to do it. Managers came up with a policy to buy them that time: Any employee who generated Web traffic would incur a $50 charge to her or his department for the month. Department managers would take notice of these charges, and employees, knowing budgets were being impacted, would be less eager to use the new technology. When management announced the policy, pandemonium ensued.

Within 24 hours, the policy generated nearly 600 email responses protesting it. Within days, top management scheduled a meeting to discuss it. People jammed the halls. People unable to show up in person linked in by satellite. Carl Meske, one of Sun's early Web users, described the meeting:

> It was standing room only...and that room will hold hundreds. All the VPs and directors were up on the stage... People were just fuming, saying, "How dare you tax us on the use of this new tool" and "I came to Sun to get away from stuff like this." It was a feeding frenzy. People felt like this is part of our job, to research and try new technologies, and for someone to stand up there and say "You can't do that, we're going to tax you to use that".... People were incensed.[6]

In the end, two network engineers came up out of the crowd and explained to all that the company really did have a network capacity problem. The mob calmed. Management rescinded the tax. Employees voluntarily reduced their Web use. Senior managers turned to other matters.

But Meske and others felt that managers didn't appreciate the importance of the new technology and started thinking of ways to get the point across. They began to work with corporate librarians to catalog and index company information in Web form. When they'd made significant progress, the small, still-volunteer team of Web enthusiasts presented their work to a group of VPs in late 1994. The meeting went badly. The VPs complained about lack of support infrastructure, management buy-in, and policies governing use of the new technology. These were real issues, recognized as such, and they turned back the charge once again.

By February 1995, the informal Web team had addressed most of the issues identified in the 1994 meeting. They got the go-ahead to announce "Sun Web" officially. Web use at Sun took another step forward when Chief Executive Officer (CEO) Scott McNealy started using it to distribute audio clips. By mid-1995, Sun had more than 1,000 Web servers, many containing sensitive company information, all managed by whoever happened to be responsible for that particular computer. By the end of that year, the number approached 2,000, 99% of them at some person's desk. At this point—two and a half years after the technology had first been used at Sun—the company launched a formal institutional initiative to manage the Web at

Sun. Finally, in the view of the company's Web fans, the Web began to get the management attention it deserved.

Not until the spring of 1996, however, did Web technology leap to the top of every senior manager's agenda. It suddenly appeared that combining the Web with a computer language called Java could yield an entirely new strategy for the company. Sun referred to the important moment these two initiatives came unexpectedly together as "The Day the Universe Changed." The company set about redefining itself from top to bottom. The technology that had been discovered and spread almost by accident took over the heart of the firm; it became central to everything at Sun.

"It was a feeding frenzy. People felt like this is part of our job, to research and try new technologies, and for someone to stand up there and say, 'We're going to tax you to use that.'... People were incensed."

ROLLING OUT WEB TECHNOLOGY AT FORD MOTOR COMPANY[7]

Ford's managers don't think of their company as an information technology (IT) company.[8] Their deliberate approach to new technologies reflects this. Ford designs, builds, sells, and services automobiles, and any new technology must add value to this core business. As a matter of corporate philosophy, the reasons for taking on any new technology must be well-understood before the company invests in it.

In late 1994, Ford CEO Alex Trotman attended an IBM Board of Directors meeting (as a member) and saw a presentation about then-new Web technologies. On his return to Ford, he asked Bill Powers, the Chief Information Officer (CIO), to create an external Web site and find other ways to use the technology. Powers established a formal organization to create the Ford Web site, which debuted in July 1995. In early 1996, Trotman asked a strategy group to develop an internal Web strategy. This staff group presented a white paper to senior management, in which they outlined ways the technology could help Ford internally and proposed a path of deployment. As a result, senior management created a larger organization, the World Wide Web Organization (WWWO), in May 1996.

The WWWO immediately established facilities and procedures for centralized, professional management of Web servers, even though the company had only a few at the time. The group developed a centralized indexing scheme for Web content, and in July 1996, it launched the "Ford Hub," the company's internal Web site home page. Efforts then turned to promoting the Web and its use. In August, WWWO staff traveled to Ford locations in the U.S. and Europe, presenting "road shows" to introduce people to the Web and describe the ways it could help them. The idea caught on, and by early 1997 there were more than 600 Web servers in use at Ford, most of them centrally managed by the WWWO.

By mid-1997, Ford managers could see the strategic importance of the Web. To facilitate connections between the company and its suppliers, Ford launched a secure business-to-business (B2B) server. Internal applications had begun to demonstrate business value. Taking full advantage of the Web would be a long-term initiative for a company the size of Ford, but these early programs established a successful trajectory.

COMPARING SUN AND FORD

When we teach these cases at Harvard Business School (HBS), we ask students to explain the differences between the stories. Figures 1–1 and 1–2 show timelines of events at the two companies; Table 1–1 contrasts features of the timelines.

Some of these contrasts are surprising. For example, two and a half years passed between the Web's first appearance at Sun and the first efforts to manage it professionally. By that time, thousands of servers were scattered all over the company, their content ensnarled in "hairballs of information."[9] Ford established a formal organization immediately, from Day One, with clearly defined objectives. Sun senior managers took even longer, nearly three years, to realize that Web technology, infiltrating the company at the grassroots level, had strategic importance. At Ford, the CEO introduced the technology, which led managers to consider it important immediately; it then rolled out formally, from the top down. The Sun

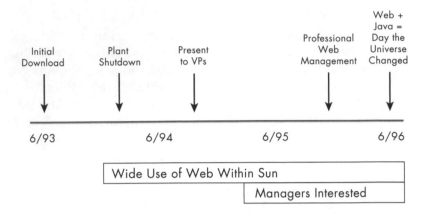

FIGURE 1–1
Timeline of events at Sun.

approach—with its cacophonous meetings and outraged employees, its trying and trying again, its managers who just didn't seem to "get it"—appears haphazard, chaotic. The Ford approach appears orderly and well-executed.

From this comparison some executives in HBS classes conclude that Ford managed well but that Sun was lucky. They give Sun little credit for managing anything. In their view, Sun's processes lacked essential structure. Without the persistence of frontline employees, Sun's managers might have missed the opportunity entirely. Probing deeper, however, they find more in these stories than a simple contrast. The Sun approach to adopting Web technology exhibits a number of interesting characteristics. For example:

- *Emphasis on emergence over planning*—Unlike Ford, Sun had no master plan for rolling out the new technology and relied instead on a decentralized, grassroots approach. No one defined project objectives in advance. The convergence of the Web project (if you could call it a "project") and the Java project on "The Day the Universe Changed" was accidental to a degree that disconcerts some executives.

- *Iterative structure*—One source of the Sun project's apparent disorderliness is the trying and trying again

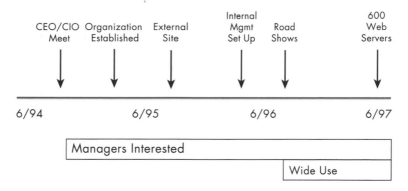

FIGURE 1-2
Timeline of events at Ford.

required to get the technology in place, in the company and in the perception of Sun's senior management. Activities overlapped, many of them uncoordinated, definitely not a case of "getting it right the first time." Periods in which people worked independently with the new technology alternated with attempts to pull things together; meeting after meeting ended without resolving the difficulties.

■ *An unusual notion of supervision and control*—Sun executives can't supervise their smart engineers in any conventional sense. This is another source of apparent

TABLE 1-1 Comparison of Sun and Ford Web Technology Deployment

SUN	FORD
Bottom up	Top down
Spontaneous deployment	Planned deployment
Formal management 2.5 years after widespread use	Formal management from the beginning
Appears haphazard	Appears expertly executed
Early adopter	Adopted one year later
"Hairballs of information" Results in a new company direction	Maximally useful information Adds value to the business

disorder. The engineers seem like *prima donnas*. It took a long time—"forever," according to the engineers—for the "suits to get it." To their credit, though, the suits know they have this difficulty and have designed a culture to accommodate and even profit from it.

■ *Getting things "wrong" a lot*—There are many "wrong" choices on the way to each useful choice. Sun's corporate history includes a long line of "wrong" strategic assertions and choices (e.g., UNIX workstations will replace PCs; network computers will replace PCs). Sun's process seems inefficient. But Sun executives have faith in their way of working, faith that they will move through "wrong" choices quickly enough to emerge with valuable ones. They know that goals and priorities will shift, and their methods are designed to roll with those changes and still "get it right before the deadline." Indeed, even while making their "wrong" choices, the company somehow continued to prosper.[10]

One class of executives at HBS came up with a useful metaphor for comparing the firms' approaches. Fittingly, it is an automotive metaphor. Ford, focused on the core business, drives cautiously. It's as if the company travels down a dark road, fearful of what might leap out of the blackness. To be safe, Ford drives deliberately, carefully, so that the car can stop in time to avoid obstacles. Sun, on the other hand, drives fast. Its road is equally dark, but Sun's managers do not see caution as an option in the uncertain computer business. Although obstacles can appear out of the night for Sun just as they can for Ford, Sun routinely overdrives its headlights. It must, therefore, routinely contend with obstacles, and to do that, it must invest in its *ability to swerve*. The company's management style thrives in situations where you can't know where you might need to turn in the future.

Sun routinely overdrives its headlights. It must, therefore, routinely contend with obstacles, and to do that, it must invest in its ability to swerve.

Investing in an ability to swerve, to devise new responses to unanticipated business situations, clearly encourages creativity. But there's more to it than that. We aim to show you that Sun's methods and processes are in fact like those of collaborative artists. To do this, we move from the hive of cubicles in Silicon Valley and the office complexes of Detroit to the old public library building in Malvern, Pennsylvania.

We enter a big room, full of light from tall windows on three sides, cluttered with odds and ends of furniture, the shiny old floor marked with stripes of colored adhesive tape. At one side sits a desk. At the desk are the play's director with a yellow legal pad and a cup full of pens, the stage manager with her kit of emergency supplies and a copy of the script, and the assistant stage manager with her script and pile of copied floor plans on which she will record the movement of the actors. The actors themselves straggle into the room with coffee cups, newspapers, rehearsal clothes, and other paraphernalia. They quietly stretch, warm up, and ready themselves for the day's work.

STREETCAR AT THE PEOPLE'S LIGHT AND THEATRE COMPANY[11]

A Streetcar Named Desire, by Tennessee Williams, is a demanding play. It's long, and difficult for the performers to sustain the energy necessary to carry it off. Many people "know" the play, mostly from a 1951 film directed by Elia Kazan, starring Marlon Brando and Vivien Leigh. This creates an obligation to offer something new in production. Everybody expects to see Brando as Stanley and Leigh as Blanche. The actors playing these roles must somehow honor *and* overcome these preconceptions.

As People's Light entered its third week of rehearsal, a lot was still up in the air. The director, nominal supervisor of the group, was grappling with the visual appearance of several key scenes. The setting had been designed to move to another theatre, one with a very shallow stage; arranging the characters in this cramped space gave her some interesting problems. The actors playing Mitch and Stanley had their own tasks. The Mitch actor was 44 years old; the Stanley actor 32. No one could ignore this difference, and the two were struggling with questions of why Stanley would be great pals with such an older guy and what form their friendship should take. The two had devised an elaborate back story (not in the script) about the army life that had made them fast friends, but they hadn't yet invented the present-time effects of that history.

Everybody knew that some things weren't coming together: Mitch and Stanley's friendship; the struggle between Blanche and the asylum people at the end; and the poker night. The group ran through each of these scenes repeatedly, everyone working simultaneously on their respective difficulties, reacting to each others' ideas and reactions. Still, the rehearsals didn't jell.

During the week, the director tinkered with the stage arrangement, moving actors here and there. Each change required myriad new choices from the actors and kept them busy in productive ways. One day, during the poker game, Mitch came up behind Stanley in his chair and pounced a half-nelson on him, pinning him at the table. The director was in the middle of thinking about something else but looked up when she heard an angry shout. Stanley struggled but couldn't get up. Everyone in the room saw the possibilities for a whole new relationship, a physical contest between the old dog and the pup that could bring new life to scene after scene.

Stanley put considerable energy into getting back at Mitch, establishing his superiority. Mitch never accepted that. The resulting horseplay got over the top from time to time, but everyone, including the director, who took notes but didn't interfere, understood how valuable this scuffling could be when worked into the gradually forming play. Mitch, as a partial result of this male-to-male violence, finally got it that his last visit to Blanche is an attempted rape, and began behaving that way. This big change in Blanche's usually gentle scene partner shocked her and moved her to a new level of terror and impending madness. The scene between them at last burst into life and began to prepare for the famous final rape.

> One day, Mitch came up behind Stanley in his chair and pounced a half-Nelson on him. The director was in the middle of something else but looked up when she heard an angry shout. Stanley struggled. Everyone in the room saw possibilities for a whole new relationship, a physical contest that could bring new life to scene after scene.

All these and other factors came together one afternoon. For example, the aftermath of the drunken poker night had always seemed like a letdown. This time through, Stella finally let herself go into the blissed-out lethargy of waking up the morning after her violent bout of fighting and sex with Stanley. Her new energy forced Blanche into busy reaction. Blanche's increasingly desperate efforts to shock her sister out of this state brought the scene to higher levels of intensity.

Other actors made similar advances that afternoon. Of course, there were glitches here and there: Actors now and then forgot a line or stumbled on an unfamiliar move. But even the glitches had new life. When one actor forgot a prop, another found it on a chair and tossed it to him; he caught it smoothly and the scene went along without a pause.

Other actors, sitting at the edges of the room when they weren't onstage, watched closely. The director took notes as fast as she could. Scribbling and whispering to her assistant, she reconceived the play-to-be as it grew before her eyes. When Stanley cleared the dinner table with a roaring sweep of his arm, the two women on stage cringed in fear. So did everyone else in the room. When Mitch grabbed Blanche and tore open her robe, the room audibly gasped. The gasp turned to real horror as Blanche sagged and almost gave in before finding one last shred of self-protective energy and shouting, "Fire!" When Stella burst into the tears described as *"luxurious"* in the stage directions, even the director had to get a grip. Something big was happening. Something beyond work came into the room.

> To understand artful approaches requires turning the focus knob of a figurative microscope to bring into the foreground, not the external symptoms and discrete *parts* that our industrial metaphors predispose us to notice, but rather those *qualities* of work that artists know and use.

The stage manager called, "And, lights." There followed a moment of hush, a deep and happy silence of accomplishment. Then, from someone in a far corner of the room came a burst of simulated static followed by the flat, empty drawl of NASAspeak: "Ahhh, Houston? We have play."

COMPARING SUN AND PEOPLE'S LIGHT

We see structural similarities between the *Streetcar* ensemble and Sun's people as they circle around and converge on a new strategy. Both work processes rely on emergence, iterative structure (trying and trying again), an unusual notion of supervision and control, and getting a lot of things "wrong" on the way to high-quality choices. More important than these structural similarities, though, are other factors that emerge when we view these examples through an artful lens: the importance of individuals' efforts to release themselves from restraining preconceptions and inhibiting circumstances; the intensity and interdependency of these collaborations; the understanding of "wrong" choices as advances rather than setbacks; the sense of the emerging product as something better and more interesting than anything a single person could have preconceived, greater than the sum of its parts; an unpredictable result that in retrospect seems inevitable.

Here lies the most important reason for managers to understand the methods of collaborative artists. It's not that traditional managers can't notice and emulate things like an iterative process structure. But to capture the full power of such processes requires understanding at a different level. It requires turning the focus knob of a figurative microscope to bring into the foreground, not the external symptoms and discrete *parts* that our industrial metaphors predispose us to notice, but rather those *qualities* of work that artists know and use. If we don't shift our focus this way, we risk reproducing the surface features of successful knowledge work without capturing its essence.

For years, Toyota has provided tours of its plants to executives from other companies, fully exposing and explaining the famous Toyota Production System. Many of these executives have returned to their own companies determined to reproduce the system faithfully. They count the same things, espouse the same principles, and so on. But as Toyota seems to realize, very few of their visitors come away with a true understanding about what is different about their system. Hence, Toyota has little fear that their methods will be used successfully to compete with them.

We want to help you see business processes through an artful making lens that looks beyond the surface features of artful collaboration to tap into the kind of on-cue innovation that theatre companies achieve routinely. To accomplish this, we'll introduce a framework for organizing our thinking, for establishing new categories that we use to conceptualize productive activities and performance.

THE FOUR QUALITIES OF ARTFUL MAKING (AN ARTFUL FRAMEWORK)

What did "We have play" mean at the end of that *Streetcar* rehearsal? Was the work done? Rehearsals over? No. Two and a half more weeks of rehearsal and a couple of previews remained before opening night. And then, since there's no way to package a play, put it on a shelf, and bring it out for performance, the company would make it again for each night of the run.

When the actor said, "We have play," he meant that the cast's work of making an ensemble, a working group whose product is greater than the sum of its parts, had achieved its first success. The new thing in the room was *Ensemble*, one of the four qualities of artful making, and the most important step in creating the work of theatre art we call a play.

Here are the four qualities that we propose for artful making, each followed by a preliminary definition. These essential features of artful making, their relationships with each other, and their applications to work will emerge as we go along. In the body of the book, we'll discuss them all, and at the book's end we'll use them to gather up an understanding of artful making that will come together as a conception of work and working, a way to think about what you do.[12]

- *Release*—The first (and perhaps the most counter-intuitive) quality of artful making, essential to the other qualities. A method of control that accepts wide variation within known parameters. Release contrasts with *restraint*, the usual method of industrial control.

- *Collaboration*—The quality exhibited by conversation, in language and behavior, during which each party, released from vanity, inhibition, and preconceptions, treats the contributions of other parties as material to make with, not as positions to argue with, so that new and unpredictable ideas emerge.

- *Ensemble*—The quality exhibited by the work of a group dedicated to collaboration in which individual members relinquish sovereignty over their work and thus create something none could have made alone: a whole greater than the sum of its parts.

- *Play*—The quality exhibited by a production while it is playing for an audience; or, the quality exhibited by interaction among members of a business group, and ultimately between the group and the customer.

As we've said, these qualities require discussion before they can become tools for fashioning new ideas about work. *Play* especially requires a step-by-step approach to understanding, and a conceptual leap to the idea of the product as an interaction between maker and customer.[13] We introduce the four qualities here so that they and the way they fit together can begin to take shape as you apply them to your situation.

UNDERSTANDING ARTFUL MAKING

In the coming chapters, we will further explain the changes an artful making lens portends in modern organizations. As we do this, we'll also answer questions that have recently been raised in areas of business where managers and workers have invented and embraced artful methods.

For example, we'll explain the specific factors and cost conditions which lead to the growing prominence of artful making at this time in history. We will identify the prerequisites that must be in place before it makes sense to take an artful making approach; in many situations, industrial making still serves very well and it would be unwise to apply artful making. We will point out similarities between evolving methods in apparently unrelated business areas and demonstrate how the artful making metaphor conceptually unites them. We will show that artful approaches are not mysterious, or flaky or fiscally irresponsible; that they are in fact learnable, rigorous, and reliable.

In the ensuing chapters, we'll often use software development as an example of modern knowledge work. Software developers, particularly those who follow so-called "agile" practices, have wrestled extensively with the challenges of artful making; their efforts provide insight into how artful making can be successful in business. But this book is not about software development. We focus at times on agile software development because it suggests what is to come in much of knowledge work. As we shall see, the signs of change are already emerging in vastly different business areas, from strategy making to managing and financing large-scale projects and ventures.

ENDNOTES

1. Original use of this phrase to describe the materials of knowledge work was by Frederick P. Brooks, Jr. in "No Silver Bullet: Essence and Accidents of Software Engineering," *IEEE Computer*, 20, no. 4 (April 1987) pp. 10–19.

2. Personal communication with the authors, Summer 2002.

3. In fact, artistic license depends on fiscal responsibility. Only when a theatre is doing a good job on the fiscal side does it have freedom on its artistic side. If a theatre fails to balance income and expenses, it goes under. No class of business enterprise we know has more skill than some theatres at squeezing a dollar for maximum effect. That sound you hear in the hallways is the eagle screaming.

4. For example, the JavaStation rollout within Sun, a consequence of the artful events described here, was much more industrial in its approach.

5. The information in this section is drawn from Mark Cotteleer and Robert D. Austin, "Sun Microsystems: Realizing the Business Value of Web Technologies" (Harvard Business School case no. 198-007, 1998).

6. Quoted in Cotteleer and Austin, "Sun Microsystems: Realizing the Business Value of Web Technologies" (Harvard Business School case no. 198-007, 1998) p. 4.

7. The information in this section is drawn from Robert D. Austin and Mark Cotteleer, "Ford Motor Company: Maximizing the Business Value of Web Technologies" (Harvard Business School case no. 198-006, 1998).

8. During the reign of Jac Nasser as CEO, from late 1998 to late 2001, the company's managers did begin to talk enthusiastically about the role of IT and the Internet in the company's success; this ended with Nasser's ouster.

9. Cotteleer and Austin, "Sun Microsystems: Realizing the Business Value of Web Technologies" (Harvard Business School case no. 198-007, 1998) p. 7.

10. As we write, Sun faces business challenges that result from the technology market meltdown of 2000–01. Whether they emerge from this period still successful will depend, we believe, on whether they are able to do now what they have done so well in the past—develop and exploit emerging strategies.

11. This episode is based on real events in 1984, in a performance in which Lee played Mitch and that Rob attended. We offer the story as an instance of a common pattern in rehearsal process.

12. As a convention throughout this book, we will capitalize Release, Collaboration, Ensemble, and Play when we mean them as qualities of artful making. When we mean them as simple verbs ("to release") or nouns ("an ensemble"), we will not.

13. This idea is not new, but it is difficult to use. W. Edwards Deming's notion of a satisfied customer employs this idea, as do more recently Pine, Gilmore, and Pine; B. Joseph Pine, James H. Gilmore, and B. Joseph Pine II, *The Experience Economy* (Boston: Harvard Business School Press, 1999). The idea is difficult because of our historical attachment to industrial metaphors that conceive "the product" as something physical to package and sell as a discrete item. Further confusion sometimes results from failure to recognize that an artful process may create a product that may subsequently be copied with industrial methods, put in a box, and sold.

2 ARTFUL MAKING RELIES ON EMERGENCE

Sun's managers and employees might see something they recognize (and like) in the way the People's Light and Theatre Company Artistic Director, Abigail Adams, does her work:

> My directing style is based on what the actors are bringing to rehearsal, and on making what you make out of those particular actors then and there. You discover the play throughout the process. I really never have an idea about what I can do or can't do. As a director, I'm keeping the actors company, I'm helping to give them courage on their journey and sometimes, roughly, I know what the journey is. Sometimes I don't. But I'm not on the journey with them. If one actor makes a choice that makes the other actor's choice impossible, then I'm there to negotiate that. But usually we try a scene or a moment so many different ways that the right choice makes itself known. And everybody in the room knows what that right choice is. We work until we find that.[1]

People's Light has become known for this style of play making, in which the product is not preconceived, but rather emerges from the process of making. Actors make choices about character, action, gesture, tone of voice, etc., which combine into an evolving form. Visiting directors sometimes use more prescriptive, command-and-control-based approaches.

But the directors and actors who are part of the People's Light resident company, like engineers at Sun, have become accustomed to working in their particular way. Such heavy reliance on emergent processes may seem like an odd way to produce a product under a firm deadline. Yet the artists at People's Light do it successfully again and again.

THE PEOPLE'S LIGHT WAY OF WORKING

There are several things to notice about Adams's approach. First, she intentionally avoids preconceived notions of the play as she enters the process of making it. Rather than trying to get the production to conform to a preconception, she orchestrates the creation of a play that will be a direct function of the available materials, the actors most significant among these. The play that results from the work of a particular company of actors will be different from one that might emerge if there were a substitute for even one of those actors. Adams enters early rehearsals with ideas about how things might go, but she deliberately avoids defining her notions in detail. Her process emphasizes immediately reconceiving everything in response to what she sees as newly possible with each passing moment of rehearsal, as a result of each new thing tried. This brings us to the second important thing to notice.

In this way of working, there's an assumption that each scene in the play will be tried "so many different ways" that high-quality choices will appear. The entire process supports trying things many times in many ways. Most of what is tried will not end up as overtly visible in the product. As at Sun, managers and workers will be "wrong" in many of their choices—although characterizing choices as "wrong" is not helpful to the process (and is, in fact, avoided in both settings).

> Adams's process emphasizes immediately reconceiving everything in response to what she sees as newly possible with each passing moment of rehearsal, as a result of each new thing tried.

In the collaborative process that is a rehearsal, every

choice an actor makes enters the play and, in some form or other, remains there. Actions become experience, and experience becomes the material that future choices are made of. Our *Streetcar* story from Chapter 1 offers an example. Suppose the director decided that Mitch's attack on Stanley couldn't really fit into the play. She could tell the men to cut it, and they would. But the older actor would not forget how one day he had nailed the younger; the younger actor would not forget how one day he'd been unfairly tricked and made to appear weaker than the old guy. People are people, and they don't have Delete keys; to some extent, including past experience in future choices is inevitable in any setting, business or art. But theatre practice embraces this fact as part of a way of working. Mitch's choice and Stanley's response, though no longer themselves visible parts of the play, are expected, encouraged even, to influence later choices. Inclusion of past actions into the materials of creation is the force that drives emergence.[2]

THE PEOPLE'S LIGHT AND THEATRE COMPANY

The People's Light and Theatre Company of Malvern, Pennsylvania, the site of much of the field research that is the basis of this book, supports an artistic company, a technical staff, and a business office with a total payroll of about 80 people and an annual cash flow of $3–5 million. People's Light produces 6–9 plays a year for about 75,000 audience members, selling tickets by subscription and singly. In addition, the theatre produces programs in education and community service; operates a function room for meetings, weddings, voting machines, and other celebrations; supports an on-site restaurant; manages a multi-acre theatre complex; and maintains a dozen small apartments to house actors and staff. It is, in fact, many businesses—arts development, entertainment, telemarketing, education, real estate, and restaurant management, to name only a few, many of which must be kept running at a profit. As we write, in the midst of an economic downturn, subscriptions at People's Light are up by 13%, total audience attendance is up 12%, earned income is up 19%, and the company has successfully completed a $9.3 million capital campaign.

NOT QUITE EXPERIMENT, NOT QUITE DISCOVERY

Business researchers have noted the advantages of cheap and rapid experimentation in situations that call for discovery or improvement, or are characterized by high uncertainty.[3] But rehearsals at People's Light are not experiments—not exactly—nor were the exploratory forays into Web use at Sun experiments—not exactly.

In rehearsal at People's Light and in new technology exploration at Sun, trying "so many different ways" isn't experimentation because these activities deliberately violate precepts of sound experimentation. For example, they don't predefine the range of possibilities to be tried. Indeed, the range of things that might be tried in rehearsal changes continuously.

Scientific experiments look for causal relationships between well-defined independent variables and dependent (outcome) variables, while seeking to hold other factors constant (or at least measuring them to see if they matter). A good experiment executes an algorithm that systematically explores a well-defined space. Rehearsal and exploration activities at Sun don't abide by detailed definitions of spaces. They remake the parameters and many other aspects of the situation with each repetition. They redraw the space even as they explore it.

This constantly changing conception of the problem, this relatively unstructured exploration of an evolving space, is well-suited to problems that involve significant ambiguity. It's a good approach to situations in which no one knows in advance the right questions to ask. The People's Light rehearsal process creates the questions, even the form of the problem itself, as the work proceeds. Questions and spaces emerge. In our interviews, artful makers at People's Light rejected the metaphor of experimentation as an inadequate description of their process. The term "experiment" is sometimes used very informally in business, to include less structured and more creative acts. Often it is framed as a general approach to problem-solving. But even in this context, we can see the difficulty that artful makers have with the word: Where did the problem come from? Does experimentation include making (defining) the problem itself? In the end, we decided that the baggage associated with the word "experiment" made it less than helpful in describing artful processes, whether in theatre or in business. People's Light artists prefer the word "creation."

Those same artists argue that the word "discover" isn't quite right either, although Adams uses the word for lack of a better one. "Discover" suggests there is a right choice waiting to be found, that rehearsal is a sort of treasure hunt, a matter of turning over the right rock. But the choices a theatre ensemble seeks do not exist in advance; they don't wait under a rock to be discovered. The actors invent them in rehearsal. The choices, the actions, and the play are created anew with each iteration. There is not one right choice you can see or imagine in advance. There are instead many high-quality, interdependent choices. They all lead to different products (some more valuable than others). Likewise, in business there is rarely a single right way to do something, a single solution waiting to be discovered. Often business people too must *make* their solutions; they won't find them waiting, ready-made.

> The choices an ensemble makes do not exist in advance; they don't wait to be "discovered." The choices, the actions, and the play are created entirely anew with each iteration.

The "not quite experimental" nature of artful making is an important strength of the approach as we attempt innovation. Ironically, this strength arises from the promise within our "mistakes"—or rather, within what might be viewed as mistakes in a structured experiment. Lewis Thomas provides insight into how getting things wrong interacts vitally with making processes, and how making is different from discovering, as he describes how computers operate differently than people do:

> Computers are good at seeing patterns, better than we are. They can connect things that seem unrelated to each other, scanning the night sky or the stained blotches of 50,000 proteins on an electrophoretic gel or the numbers generated by all the world's stock markets, and find relationships

that matter. We do something like this with our brains, but we do it differently; we get things wrong. We use information not so much for its own sake as for leading to thoughts that really are unrelated, unconnected, patternless, and sometimes, therefore, quite new. If the human brain had not possessed this special gift, we would still be sharpening bones, muttering to ourselves, unable to make up a poem or even whistle.[4]

The experimental imperfections in the artful making approach are a primary source of innovation, a vital part of making anew. Artful makers respect and even treasure their "mistakes."

EXPLORATION AND EFFICIENCY

David Bradley, a resident director at People's Light, further explains the process of rehearsal with an analogy to painting:

It's like Picasso's *Guernica*. He did tons of elaborate color sketches and renderings that are works of art themselves. He did all of that exploration, and then did a black and white painting. Sometimes the process requires you to throw yourself out there, really explore all the colors...then strip it all away to what's essential.[5]

Like Adams, Bradley describes a process that combines exploration and production. As Picasso created *Guernica*, he was developing, but he was also producing, making. This is a trademark characteristic of artful making, that it combines, at least to some degree, development and production. There may be phases of production that come after artful making in which industrial making takes over. An industrial process generates reproductions of *Guernica* for college students' dorm room walls. But, as we shall see, there are many examples, in both theatre and business, in which developing and producing are part of each other, inseparable.

Picasso's way of working on *Guernica* might seem inappropriate as an analogy for business. How can it be efficient

(cost-effective) to make so many throwaway copies on the way to the final outcome? This is the very complaint that executives in classes at HBS lodge against Sun's process for adopting Web technologies. It took Sun's senior managers a year and a half   Artful makers respect and even treasure their "mistakes."
to realize that the technology
was not some sort of video game, two and a half years to con-clude that they needed to manage Web infrastructure profes-sionally, and three years to understand the technology's tremendous strategic importance. Ford considered the technol-ogy strategically important right away and professionally man-aged the infrastructure from the beginning, albeit with the advantage of starting a year later (a more fully developed Web displayed more obvious advantages). Why did it take Sun so long? Why did they have to go through so many cycles of not getting it right? Why did Picasso?

In artful making, you can't skip to the end. Just as a swim-mer trying to reach a new level of endurance by swimming until he or she hits the wall at lap 65 must grind through 50 before getting to the 15 that condition his or her body, actors and other artful makers must move through all the necessary steps on the way to closure. Some of these steps can be very hard indeed. It's no fun swimming lap 51 (52, 53...), but you must on the way to higher performance.

Not being able to skip to the end doesn't mean the process is unreliable or inefficient. It's true that, unlike many business processes that need reliability, artful rehearsal is not disci-plined by an objective well defined in advance (except a very general objective of getting to something good before opening night). But neither is the process limited by preconceived objectives; it can produce a better result than anyone could imagine. And the lack of a detailed objective doesn't rule out reliability. People's Light routinely hits its deadlines, more reli-ably than most businesses. It's true that rehearsals don't end unexpectedly early by discovering unanticipated efficiencies. They also never run longer than planned. The play will be mounted in five weeks' time, and the play will almost always please its customers.

Like senior managers at Sun, Adams and other directors at People's Light have faith that their process will deliver valuable results on time. Their confidence in the process is based on the design of the process itself, which assures that the ensemble will have time for the first 50 laps, and that the progress of the last 15 will emerge.

EMERGENCE IN BUSINESS

The idea that some actions in business cannot be predicted but must emerge from a process, especially in conditions of high uncertainty, is supported by management research on strategy making. For example, Mintzberg and McHugh have documented the success of "grassroots" strategy formation that's completely consistent with the notion of artful making. Consider this brief passage from their article in a leading journal of management research:

> Strategies grow like weeds in a garden; they are not cultivated like tomatoes in a hothouse. . . . sometimes it is more important to let pattern emerge than to force an artificial consistency. . . . Sometimes an individual actor . . . creates his or her own pattern . . .; other times, the external environment imposes a pattern . . .; in some cases, many different actors converge around a theme, perhaps gradually, perhaps spontaneously; or sometimes senior managers fumble into strategies. . . . To manage this process is not to preconceive strategies, but to recognize their emergence and intervene when appropriate. . . . To manage in this context is to create the climate within which a wide variety of strategies can grow . . . to watch what does in fact come up and not be too quick to cut off the unexpected . . .[6]

In artful making, you can't skip to the end. But not being able to skip to the end doesn't mean the process is unreliable or inefficient.

These remarks agree with the conclusions of other researchers, some of whom apply the same ideas beyond the boundaries of strategy into fields such as product development.[7] Their findings validate the relevance and importance of emergent ideas and actions in business, even if they do not fully explain when and under what conditions such ideas could apply to other areas.

The similarities and analogous patterns in disparate areas of activity—strategy making, agile software development, theatre practice—lead us to conclude that all are specific examples of a general phenomenon we call artful making. This phenomenon is not new; it has been well understood in the theatre and other collaborative arts for centuries. But it is, for some economic reasons we'll look at, newly important in the 21st Century.

The arts give us the best models for understanding this newly important phenomenon. Business people, especially in certain areas such as agile software development, are coming around to their own sense of artful making and what it implies. But we'd all be better off to adopt the most well-developed lens available.

Like it or not, artists have something useful to say to business people. Let's get used to that. And use it.

ENDNOTES

1. Abigail Adams as quoted in Robert D. Austin, "The People's Light and Theatre Company" (Harvard Business School case no. 600-055, 2000).

2. In the event, Stanley often managed to break the hold and get out of his chair. This contest continued through the run, every night different, never predictable.

3. For example, Stefan H. Thomke, "Enlightened Experimentation: The New Imperative for Innovation," *Harvard Business Review* (February 2001).

4. "Neurology," from *The Youngest Science; Notes of a Medicine-Watcher*, by Lewis Thomas, 1983. Used by permission of Viking Penguin, a division of Penguin Putnam, Inc. pp. 89-90.

5. David Bradley, as quoted in Robert D. Austin, "The People's Light and Theatre Company" (Harvard Business School case no. 600-055, 2000).

6 Henry Mintzberg and Alexandra McHugh, "Strategy Formation in an Adhocracy," *Administrative Science Quarterly*, 30, no. 2 (June 1985) pp. 160–197.

7. For example, James Brian Quinn, *Strategies for Change: Logical Incrementalism* (Homewood, IL: Irwin, 1980); Richard M. Cyert and James G. March, *A Behavioral Theory of the Firm* (Englewood Cliffs, NJ: Prentice-Hall, 1963); Richard T. Pascale, "Perspectives on Strategy: The Real Story Behind Honda's Success," *California Management Review*, 26, no. 3 (1984) pp. 47–72; Kathleen M. Eisenhardt, "Making Fast Strategic Decisions in High-Velocity Environments," *Academy of Management Journal*, 32, no. 3 (1989) p. 543; and Kathleen M. Eisenhardt and Benham N. Tabrizi, "Accelerating Adaptive Processes: Product Innovation in the Global Computer Industry," *Administrative Science Quarterly*, 40, no.1 (1995) pp. 84–110.

3 ARTFUL MAKING IS ITERATIVE, NOT SEQUENTIAL

It's useful (though simplistic) to say that industrial making processes tend to be linear, or *sequential*, while artful making processes tend to be helical, or *iterative*. Figure 3–1 compares a classic, sequential industrial making process for making cars with an artful making iteration for making software.

AUTO MAKING: MOSTLY INDUSTRIAL

In auto making, you must plan before doing because it's expensive to make changes. Changes to the product design in the middle of process engineering, for example, could require retooling in the assembly plant and in suppliers' plants. Early changes can also run up costs because of ripple effects across the project. For example, if you move the battery to a new location, you may have to figure out an alternate route for engine coolant. Consequently, automakers often portray their making process as a sequence of major activities that move from planning to assembling. Thorough analysis early in a project prevents, or at least minimizes, the high cost of late changes.[1]

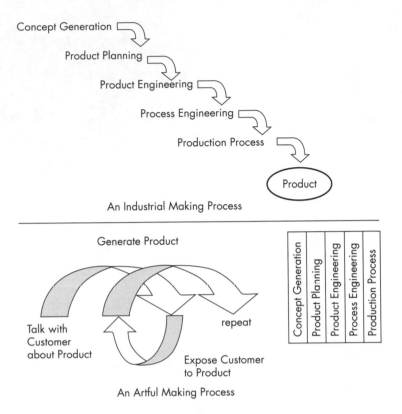

FIGURE 3–1
Comparing the shapes of industrial and artful making.[2]

In practice, car making is not completely sequential. It includes "loops, parallel steps, and obscure boundaries"[3] that introduce exploration and in-process learning to complement up-front analysis. But the tasks of car making have distinct boundaries. Tasks in product engineering differ from those in process engineering, which in turn differ from those in the production process. Often these tasks involve different people (though in many organizations, all work together at least some of the time); different organizations take responsibility for each activity (although sometimes responsibilities fall to hybrid organizations, such as "cross-functional teams"). Product Development and Manufacturing are often separate business units and may be housed in separate buildings. Almost always, these distinct entities produce distinct outputs. The product design, which formally specifies the desired end-product, is distinct from the process design, which describes how the product will be made.[4]

SOFTWARE MAKING AT TRILOGY: MOSTLY ARTFUL

In contrast to *sequential* methods for making cars, software development methods can be arranged so that changes are relatively inexpensive. It's inherently easier to change symbols recorded in an electronic file than it is to bend metal, but that's not the whole story. Cheap and rapid changes require enabling technologies such as version control systems (which allow developers to roll back changes) and automated testing systems (which allow quick assessment of the impacts of changes), not to mention continuous building of design skills. Given appropriate investments in technologies and design skills, software development, like many other knowledge work processes, can become *iterative* and less dependent on planning.

Trilogy, a Texas software company, uses such a cheap and rapid *iterative* process, their "Fast Cycle Time" methodology. Trilogy developers rapidly generate rough prototypes. They give their customers something to respond to quickly and often. Even if prototypes

As developers work rapidly through iterations, they perform many tasks similar to those in the automaker's sequential process. But they turn the sequential process on its ear, hitting each of the tasks in parallel or in rapid succession.

differ wildly from what customers had in mind, developers gain rich information from customer responses. Scott Snyder, Trilogy's chief of development, put it this way: "Customers will say, 'Uh-uh, this isn't what I want, but if I could just do *that* with *this* screen it would be awesome.'"[5] Trilogy's programmers act quickly on customer suggestions and generate another product version. Then they repeat the cycle. They speed through many iterations, each of which allows for adjustments. When you can run this process fast enough, often enough, and cheaply enough (more about this in the next chapter), it makes little sense to plan extensively or create detailed specifications before you begin doing. If "aim-fire-adjust" works fast enough, you can move beyond "ready-aim-fire."[6]

As Trilogy works rapidly through iterations, it performs many tasks similar to those in the automaker's sequential process. Trilogy's developers get new ideas (concept generation), figure out what the product ought to do and how it ought to do it (product planning and engineering), decide how to make it (process engineering), and make one (production) every time they loop through their cycle. But they turn the sequential development process on its ear, hitting each of the tasks in parallel or in rapid succession, intermingling them.

This yields flexibility benefits. If the customer wants a change in the midst of development, the iterative process can quickly improvise an accommodation. Management researchers Alan MacCormack and Marco Iansiti have documented this iterative method and characterized its benefits as they appear in a wide range of software development organizations.[7] Proponents of the agile software development movement have long advocated iterative structures.[8] The flexibility that results from this approach isn't completely due to Trilogy's wisdom. The natural characteristics and cost structures of software development (shared by many other kinds of knowledge work) are prerequisite and fertile ground for this kind of management.

The iterative shape of artful making resonates beyond product development. As we have seen, strategy making is another area in which management scholars have observed iterative, emergent processes.[9] Figure 3–2 depicts the iterative strategy making approach followed by Sun Microsystems as that company maneuvered through unpredictable competitive and technological environments on its way to "The Day the Universe Changed."[10] Artful making can also guide efforts to manage uncertainty in many areas of business. We'll look closely at this in later chapters.

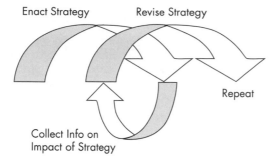

FIGURE 3–2
An artful making approach to strategy.

THE ITERATIVE STRUCTURE OF PLAY PRODUCTION

The realization that rehearsal, the primary activity of play production, has a structure similar to certain business processes, especially agile software development, launched our research project. We focused on the People's Light and Theatre Company because of its emergent approach, and because Lee's 20-year affiliation with the company provided access to work often shielded from outside observers. To be sure, other theatres operate in somewhat different ways. The emergent management and directing style of People's Light, as well as its resident company approach,[11] make it somewhat unusual. But the methods and practices in use there don't seem radical or experimental to members of other theatre communities.

THE SCRIPT IS NOT THE PLAY, NOR IS IT A SPECIFICATION

People unfamiliar with the theatre sometimes believe that the objective of play making is to do exactly what is in the script, fulfilling the author's intentions as well as possible every night of the run. If this view were correct, we could treat the script as a specification and rehearsal would be like setting up a factory. Play making doesn't work that way.

The script guides the director, designers, and actors as they create a play. It contains the words the actors will speak, and most theatres follow a rule that requires actors to say those words as written. The script usually, but not always, contains stage directions offering notes on the setting and movements of the characters, more or less detailed depending on the playwright. But the script is a wholly inadequate specification, lacking sufficient detail to control the rehearsal process the way plans and specifications control industrial processes.

Here are the first few lines of a famous script:[12]

ACT I

SCENE I

   Enter BARNARDO *and* FRANCISCO, *two Sentinels.*

Barnardo. Who's there?

Francisco. Nay, answer me. Stand and unfold yourself.

Barnardo. Long live the King!

Several versions of this script have survived the 400 years since it was written. No one knows for sure which of these most accurately represents the playwright's intentions. Those intentions, of course, are also 400 years old. Would they be of interest to an audience today? Editors usually conflate the extant scripts, putting together their own idea of a coherent version. The script contains no descriptions of place, costume, or equipment. Where are these guys? What do they look like? In the first play made from this script, the guys were on a bare platform with two big columns holding up a roof. They wore contemporary (Elizabethan) clothes and carried contemporary weapons. None of this is in these opening lines. The rest of the script features a similar lack of data.

Most of what needs to be done to make a play with this or any other script must be created entirely anew for each production. It's most useful to think of the script as material from which a company makes a play. As material, the script is the source of some constraints (materials always constrain product: If you have clay but no straw, you'd better not try to make bricks), but a play contains many other materials (including the actors and their work). Successful play making results in wide and interesting

The script is a wholly inadequate specification, lacking sufficient detail to control the rehearsal process the way plans and specifications control industrial processes.

variations among different productions, all consistent with a given script. No one involved in play making ever seeks to replicate a previous production exactly, or to conform to anything like a detailed specification.

THE WRITER'S VIEW OF THE SCRIPT

Writers occupy a strange place in play making. It's convenient and helpful to think of a script as material for a play, but playwrights take different positions on that. In the view of some, the script and play *are* essentially the same thing, and rehearsal is instrumental, not creative. Terrence McNally illustrates conflicted feelings in this matter:

> I accept that theatre is a collaboration. Edward Albee called me the other day and said, "You're such a goody-two-shoes. I just read some interview where you said theatre's a collaboration. Do you really believe that?" And I said, "Yes, I really do. And you really don't, do you?" And he said, "No, I don't."

McNally continued:

> I think being a playwright is being 100% responsible for what happens on stage, which means acknowledging what other people have done . . . It's not enough to say here's the script, I hope they'll do it right.[13]

The point here is that even the playwright is unclear about who owns the play. McNally can't entirely get rid of the sense of collaboration as something more than "Everybody do as I say." He knows that other artists make huge contributions to the play on the stage, but feels himself ultimately responsible. Albee has no such lack of clarity; he's absolutely sure about who's in charge. In fact, to produce an Albee script today a theatre must have his personal approval of cast and director.

This variety of attitudes about writing is only the first of many ambiguities that make up the given circumstances of play making. If the writer takes part in the rehearsal process, the organization must be prepared to adjust to his or her views. In this sense, too, the script is like a high-level architectural rendering, standard, or plan, in that it prescribes certain boundaries and requires certain behaviors. But those boundaries and behaviors are nowhere near as precise as the information in a blueprint or process specification.

Artful making methods and makers aren't daunted by the need to resolve such apparent constraints or conflicts of interest. As we shall see, the artful method is a conversation in which all parties come away with new ideas. For most productions of a script, of course, the playwright isn't a factor. All good scripts outlive their authors.

REHEARSAL PROCESS

Figure 3–3 depicts the structure of the rehearsal process at People's Light. Observation of the process reveals the following steps:

1. Actors individually research and prepare their roles.

2. They convene daily in rehearsal to work bits of the script into coherent pieces of the emerging play that can be considered and discussed.

3. The director and actors discuss each bit of work; the experiences of the work just completed are the primary subject.

4. The process repeats.

Individual actor preparations, done in parallel, will be inconsistent with each other, based on different assumptions about how the play will unfold. When the group members convene to try out what they've individually prepared, their efforts combine messily, providing ample evidence of the script's lack of controlling detail.

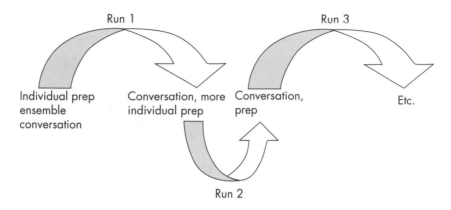

FIGURE 3–3
The rehearsal process at People's Light.

But a primary purpose of the rehearsals is, of course, to coordinate. Through repeated iteration, actors transform conflicting actions into a coherent and unified form. Such a process—uncoordinated, simultaneous, individual acts of creation punctuated by arduous episodes of bringing everything together—can seem disorganized. It can appear "poorly managed" when it is, in fact, expertly managed. Although rigorously structured by its iterative shape, rehearsal doesn't manifest an orderly appearance the way planning-based methods can.

AGILE SOFTWARE DEVELOPMENT

Agile software development has arisen independently under many different banners (e.g., Extreme Programming, Adaptive Software Development, Scrum, Dynamic Systems Development Method, Crystal, Feature-Driven Development, Pragmatic Programming), carried by proponents who don't always agree with each other on details. In February 2001, however, at The Lodge at Snowbird ski resort in the Wasatch Mountains of Utah, 17 of these banner-carriers (such as Kent Beck, Jim Highsmith, and Ken Schwaber) met to set down in writing a common core of methods and values in the work they were doing and promoting. This group agreed on "agile" as a

TABLE 3–1 The Manifesto for Agile Software Development.[14]

MANIFESTO FOR AGILE
SOFTWARE DEVELOPMENT

We are uncovering better ways of developing software
by doing it and helping others do it.
Through this work we have come to value:

Individuals and interactions	over	processes and tools
Working software	over	comprehensive documentation
Customer collaboration	over	contract negotiation
Responding to change	over	following a plan

That is, while there is value in the items on the right,
we value the items on the left more.

---

label for the family of ways of working that shared this common core. They composed several documents on agile software development; Table 3–1 reproduces the most famous of these, the "Manifesto for Agile Software Development."

The structural features of agile methods are very much like the Trilogy development process described earlier (in fact, Trilogy's CEO has said of Kent Beck's *Extreme Programming* that it describes how Trilogy develops software, even though their methods evolved independently). The most obvious characteristics shared by agile approaches are: their iterative nature; their emphasis on "early and continuous delivery of valuable software"; and their drive to "deliver working software frequently" via cheap and rapid cycles. Agile development also aims to "welcome changing requirements, even late in development."[15] Like theatre practice, agile software development centers on people and urges project leaders to "build projects around motivated individuals," "give them the environment and support they need," and "trust them to get the job done." Beck describes the software development process as "conversation,"[16] using the term in much the same sense as we do, and Jim Highsmith notes that agile approaches combine exploration and production.[17] Also, like theatre practice, the participants in agile software development must meet certain requirements, the equivalent of a script in play making, which are not nearly enough to specify the product. In software development, these requirements take forms such as: "The system must accomplish A, B, and C," or "The system must execute processes X, Y, and Z in compliance with Generally Accepted Accounting Principles (GAAP)."

We can abstract the processes of agile development into the following steps, which parallel the steps of theatre rehearsal:

1. After conversing with the customer and among themselves about what the software should do, developers write code individually or in pairs.

2. They regularly convene to build the system into an executing program that can be run and tested.

3. The customer, developers, and project leaders discuss each run; the experiences resulting from the last run are the main subject, along with ideas about change.

4. The process repeats.

Individual developer preparations, and code written in parallel may be inconsistent with each other based on different assumptions about how the system will work and what it needs. When the group convenes to test and discuss their experiences of a particular iteration of the running software, they may note that actions have combined messily, providing ample evidence of lack of coordination among individuals.

A primary purpose of the conversation is, of course, to discover where things are not coordinated and to make fixes in future iterations. Through repetitions of this cycle, developers and others on the project transform conflicting actions into a coherent form. This process, uncoordinated, simultaneous, individual acts of creation punctuated by arduous episodes of pulling everything together, can seem disorganized. It can appear "poorly managed" when it is, in fact, expertly managed. Although rigorously structured by its iterative shape, the process doesn't manifest in an orderly appearance the way planning-based methods can.

ARTFUL MAKING IN SOFTWARE
DEVELOPMENT AND THEATRE

As Table 3–2 suggests, the agile software build process parallels theatre rehearsal in a variety of ways. We suggest that these two creative processes are in fact specific cases of the same general phenomenon, artful making.

TABLE 3–2 External Characteristics of Artful Making in Agile Software Development and Play Making

	SOFTWARE DEVELOPMENT	PLAY MAKING
Iterative cycle	Product build and test	Rehearsal
Distributed, independent, simultaneous invention	Individual programmers at work on their source code	Individual actors preparing between runs
Unifying action	A product build	A rehearsal run
A director who facilitates coherent choices	The project manager	The director
Forum for conversation	Meetings, technology-based collaborative forums	The rehearsal room
Way of setting structure	Code holds structure	Actors enact structure

ITERATION AS A STRUCTURE
FOR RIGOROUS WORK

Accepting iteration as an alternative to sequential work structures involves some serious rethinking of ideas we take for granted from our industrial past. The development of enabling technologies increasingly makes iteration a possible alternative to the old ways, and the accelerating rise in the importance of knowledge work makes it essential. We'll be looking at rehearsal as a way to approach an understanding of new, artful ways of making things other than plays. In the next chapter, however, we need to take a brief look at the range of situations in which artful making can contribute, and those in which it cannot.

ENDNOTES

1. Gary P. Pisano, "BMW: The 7-Series Project (A)" (Harvard Business School case no. 692-083, 1993) provides an exploration of some of the issues involved in making late changes on product development projects in the auto industry.

2. The descriptions of phases of automaking are from *Product Development Performance*, by Kim Clark and Takahiro Fujimoto, Harvard Business School Press, Boston, MA, 1991, p. 27. The depiction of software development process is our interpretation of the "fast cycle time" software development process at Trilogy, in Austin, Texas. For more information on Trilogy's software development practices, see Robert D. Austin, "Trilogy (A)," (Harvard Business School case no. 699-034, 1999); "Trilogy (B)," (Harvard Business School case no. 600-123, 2000); and "Trilogy (C)," (Harvard Business School case no. 601-140, 2001).

3. Clark and Fujimoto (1991).

4. It has become common in recent years to structure project teams so as to develop a sense of collective, "cradle-to-grave" responsibility for a new product. These teams are often "cross-functional," meaning that the different organizations involved in the different activities are all represented. This practice blurs the lines of responsibility for different phases of an auto project, but does not eliminate them. There remains a division of labor among the representatives of different functions. For example, a tension between product engineers and manufacturing engineers, each of whom feel primary ownership for different activities, remains in most auto companies.

5. Quoted in Robert D. Austin, "Trilogy (A)" (Harvard Business School case no. 699-034, 1999) p. 9. Emphasis added.

6. Gary Hamel has often used this "ready-aim-fire versus aim-fire-adjust" metaphor. See, for example, his *Leading the Revolution* (Boston: Harvard Business School Press, 2000).

7. Alan D. MacCormack and Marco Iansiti, "Developing Products on Internet Time," *Harvard Business Review* (September–October 1997).

8. See, for example, Kent Beck, *Extreme Programming Explained: Embrace Change* (Boston: Addison-Wesley, 1999); James A. Highsmith III, *Adaptive Software Development: A Collaborative Approach to Managing Complex Systems* (New York: Dorset House, 2000); and Barry Boehm, "A Spiral Model of Software Development and Enhancement," *IEEE Computer*, 21, no. 5 (May 1988) pp. 61–72.

9. Henry Mintzberg and Alexandra McHugh, "Strategy Formation in an Adhocracy," *Administrative Science Quarterly*, 30, no. 2 (June 1985) pp. 160–197.

10. This is our interpretation of a process described by Mark J. Cotteleer and Robert D. Austin, "Sun Microsystems: Realizing the Business Value of Web Technologies" (Harvard Business School case no. 198-007, 1998).

11. Many, if not most, artists in the American professional theatre are like migrant workers. They find employment one job at a time, and they go where the work is: New York City for a movie or a commercial; Syracuse, or Minneapolis, or Atlanta for a 10-week job on a play. People's Light maintains complex, ongoing relationships with about 40 artists. Ten of these (actors, designers, and directors) are on year-round contract. Several actors serve as artistic associates, advising the artistic director. Many of the actors teach at the theatre. In addition, there's a core group of 20 artists (actors, designers, directors, and playwrights) who work regularly, though not year–round. Resident company artists are encouraged to work at other theatres, and guest actors, directors, designers, and dramaturgs join the company on a project-by-project basis. The core group remains more or less constant, providing an unusual (for an American theatre) degree of organizational continuity.

12. William Shakespeare, *Hamlet*, ed. Harold Jenkins, *The Arden Edition of the Works of William Shakespeare*, gen. ed. Richard Proudfoot (London and New York: Metheun, 1982) p. 163.

13. Copyright 1997 from *Terrence McNally, A Casebook*, ed. Toby Silverman Zinman (New York: Garland Publishing, Inc., 1997) p. 8. Reproduced by permission of Routledge, Inc., part of the Taylor & Francis Group.

14. Composed by Kent Beck, Mike Beedle, Arie van Bennekum, Alistair Cockburn, Ward Cunningham, Martin Fowler, James Grenning, Jim Highsmith, Andrew Hunt, Ron Jeffries, Jon Kern, Brian Marick, Robert C. Martin, Steve Mellor, Ken Schwaber, Jeff Sutherland, Dave Thomas, on February 11–13, 2001, The Lodge at Snowbird, a ski resort in the Wasatch Mountains of Utah.

15. *http://agilemanifesto.org/principles.html*

16. From remarks Beck made during a presentation at the Cutter Summit, April 29–May 1, 2001, Cambridge, MA.

17. From remarks Jim Highsmith made during a presentation at the Cutter Summit, April 29–May 1, 2001, Cambridge, MA.

4

THE PREREQUISITE CONDITIONS FOR ARTFUL MAKING

Artful making isn't always the right approach for creating business value. The conditions must be right for artful methods to make sense. The prerequisites are firm, no "ifs" or "maybes" about them. Following an artful making approach when prerequisite conditions are not satisfied is unwise, for reasons we explain in this chapter. As we shall see, applying industrial making approaches when the prerequisites for artful making *are* satisfied is also unwise.

ARTFUL MAKING ISN'T ALWAYS THE BEST APPROACH

Sometimes the processes of making don't need to be innovative; sometimes exact replication will do. Other times innovation *is* needed but artful making isn't feasible because prerequisite conditions are not in place. The approach you use—artful or industrial making—is not entirely a matter of choice.

Artful making features rapid and frequent iteration. You can only reasonably follow the approach when iteration—doing and doing again—is *inexpensive* relative to the benefits gained from experience. If the cost of doing is high, then doing

You can only reasonably follow an artful making approach when iteration—doing and doing again—is inexpensive relative to the benefits gained from experience.

and doing again is a bad idea; you should then prefer to spend more time planning, to make it more likely that you'll succeed on the first attempt. Industrial making provides the best approach to situations with a high cost of iteration.

To decide which approach to use, you must have an understanding of the sources of the *cost of iteration*. This cost has two components: *reconfiguration costs* and *exploration costs*, both of which must be low to support artful making.

RECONFIGURATION COSTS

When we set up a process for making something and then run that process, we get a particular outcome. If we re-run that same process without changing it, we'll get that same outcome. Changing the process so that it yields a new outcome generates a *cost of reconfiguration*. In car making, for example, reconfiguring might involve expensive retooling, buying new equipment, even changing the layout of a plant. As we have seen, reconfiguring in software development can be relatively inexpensive, given appropriate investments in enabling technologies and design skills. Theatre production arranges and rearranges the actions and interactions of the performers, also inexpensively. Hence, software development as well as other business activities can be, in this regard, more like rehearsal than like car making.

EXPLORATION COSTS

The second component of the cost of iteration is the cost of trying something that doesn't work well enough to continue doing it. In an industrial setting, we might think of exploration costs as "scrap costs." It's expensive to throw away physical prototypes. When the cost of exploration is high, you want to avoid making too many throw aways. Similarly, a doctor must consider that iteration may have unacceptable impacts on patients. Trying out different medications might have a cost measured in inconvenience or discomfort; trying and trying again in surgery might kill or maim someone. Software development, by contrast, routinely generates "bad" versions as a way to explore possibilities. These versions are not released for customer use and can be fixed as early as the next day with a new build. Here, too, software development is more like rehearsal than manufacturing; in theatre, there is not much lost when actors try something that doesn't "work" because something different can be tried in the next rehearsal.

THE GENERAL APPLICABILITY OF ARTFUL MAKING

Some business activities other than software development also have a low cost of iteration—strategy making at Sun, for instance. Much of what we call "knowledge work," when supported by appropriate enabling technologies, can be structured so that doing and doing again doesn't cost much relative to the benefits of experience. Provided there is a need for innovation in such settings, artful making is the recommended approach. Applying more industrial, planning-intensive, or goal-directed approaches in these conditions makes no sense.

Figure 4–1 shows the kinds of work for which artful making should be desirable and feasible. Many activities don't have

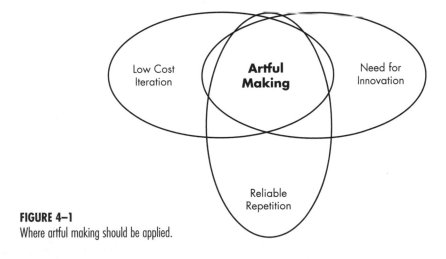

FIGURE 4–1
Where artful making should be applied.

all three of these characteristics. Recordkeeping, for example, is knowledge work that must be done repeatedly and reliably, but it usually requires little or no innovation. Solving problems stemming from the merger of two large companies is knowledge work and requires innovation, but you might not repeat it. Crafting custom jewelry products out of precious metal requires repeated and reliable innovation, but it isn't knowledge work because the materials involved are expensive to throw away or recycle, so the cost of iteration is high (you can't afford to try and try again).

THE ROLE OF ENABLING TECHNOLOGIES IN REDUCING THE COST OF ITERATION

Artful making isn't new. It's been around since the first hunting dance or primitive ritual. This way of thinking about how to change materials into a product began with the simplest fabrications; over the ages it has become more and more closely identified with works of art, products that exist simply for the sake of the pleasure they give a maker and an observer. Recently, however, business people in companies like Sun Microsystems and Trilogy have begun to see advantages in this way of working. A question that arises quite reasonably is: Why now? Why has artful making become newly relevant in the 21st Century?

We have repeatedly alluded to one reason: The new kind of work we find ourselves doing (knowledge work) has inherently different cost characteristics than physical work; it has inherently lower reconfiguration and exploration costs. But, as we have seen, there is another factor without which low iteration cost would be difficult to realize even in knowledge work: the development of *enabling technologies* that reduce reconfiguration and exploration costs. Almost always, these enabling technologies are information technologies that help

Knowledge work has inherently different cost characteristics than physical work; it has inherently lower reconfiguration and exploration costs. But, there is another factor without which low iteration cost would be difficult to realize even in knowledge work: the development of enabling technologies that reduce reconfiguration and exploration costs.

us more rapidly and cheaply reconfigure systems and explore many possibilities without incurring high costs.

REDUCING RECONFIGURATION COSTS: SOFTWARE DEVELOPMENT

In the early days of computing, writing programs (creating instructions for the machine to follow) was arduous. Often it involved setting a series of switches over and over again, each setting providing a small part of the program's instructions. It was not uncommon for a simple program to require tens of thousands of settings, which had to be applied without making a mistake or accidentally shutting off the power to the computer.[1] Only after these instructions were complete could the computer perform useful operations. Using early computers almost always involved expensive, long lead-time delays. J.C.R. Licklider, one of the pioneers of the Internet, described how computers were used in those days:

> You formulate your problem today. Tomorrow you spend with a programmer. Next week the computer devotes five minutes to assembling your program and 47 seconds to calculating the answer to your problem. You get a sheet of paper 20 feet long, full of numbers that, instead of providing a final solution, only suggest a tactic that should be explored by simulation.[2]

The problem, as Licklider expressed it, was that in ordinary intellectual work, whether assisted by computers or not, "About 85% of my 'thinking' time was spent getting into a position to think, to make decisions, to learn something I needed to know." Even then, however, the prescient Licklider realized that the computer could reduce that 85% and allow humans to spend more time on formulation, insight, learning, and improvement. To do that, though, computers had to become much easier to *reconfigure*.

The intervening years have seen much of Licklider's vision come true. In contrast to the cycle Licklider describes, that multi-day ordeal, a similar cycle can now be accomplished in minutes. Entire new versions of large software products can be built daily. Even the largest systems, if appropriately structured, can be fundamentally changed in a matter of days, weeks at most.

The use of IT to drive down the cost of reconfiguration even affects hardware-intensive realms such as manufacturing plants. Computer-controlled machines can be reconfigured between jobs much more rapidly than older, mechanically-controlled machines. Even the metal-bending world of heavy manufacturing now sees a very significant reduction in such costs, though artful making hasn't yet become the predominant approach.

REDUCING EXPLORATION COSTS: SIMULATION, PROTOTYPING, AND VERSION CONTROL

In addition to its role in lowering reconfiguration costs, IT is often applied to reduce exploration costs, the costs associated with trying something that doesn't work well enough to continue doing it. The most obvious examples are technologies used to simulate equipment or products that would be expensive to produce and try out physically. It's much cheaper to crash a virtual car in a virtual crash-test simulator than it is to crash a physical car in a physical crash-test facility. We can try out features that might have safety implications without scrapping a lot of cars. It also means that we will probably try more new things, and more new things that seem like long shots—the sort of unlikely-to-work-but-if-it-does-"Wow!" features that would never be tried in a high-cost-of-exploration environment. Many virtual experimentation systems, such as those increasingly used in drug research, provide similar advantages.[3]

Modern software development again provides a good example, especially as practiced by agile developers. Because agile developers can build and test interim products quickly, they detect problems quickly. What they can't solve, they can back out cheaply and easily. Each version of a developing system is stored in a "version control system," so it's a relatively simple matter to rewind changes. Version control allows restoration of the last version (or even an earlier version) so developers can "go with an idea" for a while (i.e., for multiple versions), safe in the knowledge that they can backtrack and try something different when they need to. When the software stabilizes to a reasonable degree, they can release a version for use by customers.

Technologies that permit rigorous and disciplined methods for testing and for migrating products into actual use by customers play a vital role in artful making. If we can't prevent changes that don't work well from negatively affecting customers, artful making won't work. Negative impacts on customers are among the most significant exploration costs. An absence of technologies to enable testing on virtual rather than real customers—in areas such as medicine, for example, where customers are patients—can, and should, inhibit artful making.

When cost conditions support artful making, competitive forces often drive companies to compete artfully.

WHEN ARTFUL AND INDUSTRIAL MAKING ARE COMBINED

As we have seen, most productive efforts combine artful and industrial making. Auto production, which we have suggested as a classic example of industrial making, has undeniably sequential and planning-intensive elements. It also has elements of artful making. On a Toyota assembly line, the parts almost always fit in accordance with the specification; on the rare occasions when they don't, a worker and others on the team must create a new solution—they must improvise. The widely admired Toyota Production System is, in fact, built on the presumption that this kind of improvisation is valuable and cost-effective.[4]

Even theatre, our main example of artful making, requires elements of industrial making. Long before rehearsals start, designers and artisans begin conceiving and constructing the not-yet-made play's setting, furnishings, costumes, sounds, and musical accompaniment, and think about ways to light it all. Since they work with physical things, these artists and artisans must make closure on their ideas in time to find, borrow, buy, rent, or construct them. The things they make become part of the rehearsal's given circumstances; they're set early on and can be changed only at great expense and difficulty. The different design elements are interdependent with each other and with the play-to-be as a whole. For instance, the set designer has chosen a color for the walls of the room, and the costumer has used this color in her palette for the clothing. Then the prop master discovers a gorgeous rug of a clashing color that the dealer will rent for a song plus a mention in the program. Do we make a change? Is there time? Will the budget allow it?

One of a director's most pressing duties is to coordinate the development and building of these designs, orchestrating combinations of work so that as they progress, they all help rather than hinder each other. They converge on to the stage in the right order, at the right time, without disrupting the more emergent rehearsal processes that proceed in parallel. The director facilitates collaboration among the various design artists or, as a last resort, makes a choice and enforces it.

How Competitive Forces Drive Work Toward Artfulness

When cost conditions support artful making, competitive forces often drive companies to compete artfully. Even in the sleepiest industry, one not traditionally characterized by innovation, enabling technologies that reduce the cost of iteration may lead to a need for artful making. Sooner or later one player in the market realizes that the new technology enables it to compete artfully, to innovate and thus differentiate the company's products or services from those of its competitors. When that happens, the competitors have two choices: (1) lose business to the more innovative competitor, or (2) apply artful methods themselves.[5] Consequently, even if you work in an industry that doesn't compete on innovation, perhaps one in which you enjoy some natural advantage (say, low labor costs), you may not be safe from the need for artful making.

This competitive dynamic generates a prediction that follows from our artful making framework: As enabling technologies continue to lower the cost of iteration, industries will increasingly compete on innovation, on their artful capabilities. Sleepy industries will wake up. Fundamental production processes will be restructured to emphasize rapid reconfiguration, that is, iteration. This is already happening in knowledge industries. Others, we believe, will follow.

Some people use the high cost of the reconfiguration that is a consequence of sequential process design as an argument to justify sequential process design. Organizations that fall prey to this circular argument are stuck in an obsolete box.

A COMMON PROBLEM: IMPOSING INDUSTRIAL COSTS ON POTENTIALLY ARTFUL PROCESSES

Iterative processes often require underlying enabling technologies to make the cost of iteration low. But these technologies do not *guarantee* low cost of iteration. To achieve a low cost of iteration may require new methods that realize the potential of enabling technologies. These new methods usually don't arise overnight and may be obstructed by organizational and cultural inertia, the usual suspects in a case of resistance to change. Proponents of industrial methods may resist the changes implied by artful process structures. Software development again provides an excellent example.

Many organizations still do their software development in a sequential manner that closely resembles an industrial making process, despite the emergence of technologies that can make development more iterative. The factory metaphor has amazing stamina. We still talk about standardizing procedures, about quality control, about software *engineering*. When we think in these categories, old process designs persist, and so do old costs. Some people use the high cost of reconfiguration, a consequence of the old sequential process design, as an argument to justify using the old process. But organizations that fall prey to this circular argument are stuck in an obsolete box. They will eventually restructure their making processes, rendering them more iterative and artful, or they won't. In the latter case they'll find themselves at a profound disadvantage.

THE HISTORICAL EVOLUTION OF ARTFUL MAKING PREREQUISITES

The conditions that require artful making didn't magically appear out of nowhere. They've been part of work, in greater or lesser degree, since work began. That doesn't mean that ideas about how to work haven't changed since ancient times, or that they don't need to develop and change now, to keep up with technology, and with changes in the way we think about work and creativity. The conditions that bear on artful making prerequisites evolve like anything else.

To understand how these conditions evolve, and how, therefore, ideas about work ought also to evolve—to answer the question of why artful making is taking on greater importance at this point in history—we'll take a brief look at its historical context. Viewed properly, artful making can be seen as an inevitable outcome of the transition from an industrial to an information economy, just as industrial making was the inevitable outcome of the transition from an agrarian to an industrial economy. In the next chapter, we will demonstrate how the changes suggested by artful making are related, through cost of iteration, to changes that occurred in the past. It's a big jump from, say, a medieval arms manufactory powered by a water-driven wheel to a high-tech software firm, but the line of development is discernible. Interestingly, the medieval armor maker had some ideas about work that we find newly useful today.

ENDNOTES

1. For a detailed account of how early computers were programmed and operated, see Paul Freiberger and Michael Swaine, *Fire in the Valley: The Making of the Personal Computer, Collector's Edition* (Boston: McGraw-Hill, 1999).

2. J.C.R. Licklider, "Man-Computer Symbiosis," *IRE Transactions on Human Factors in Electronics*, HFE-1 (March 1960) pp. 4–11.

3. See Michael Schrage's *Serious Play: How the World's Best Companies Simulate to Innovate* (Boston: Harvard Business School Press, 2000).

4. H. Kent Bowen and Steven Spear, "Decoding the DNA of the Toyota Production System," *Harvard Business Review* (September 1999).

5. In some markets, there can be a third option, something like: exert market power, litigate, or lobby government officials to prevent competitors' innovations from capturing economic value.

5 ARTFUL MAKING AS PART OF THE SHIFT TO A KNOWLEDGE ECONOMY

In the previous chapter, we identified prerequisite conditions in which artful making approaches should be used, and suggested that, thanks to enabling information technologies, these prerequisites are increasingly prevalent in business. In this chapter, we will continue that discussion in a historical context, for two reasons. First, viewing artful making this way adds weight to the notion that it is part of the shift from an industrial to an information economy. Second, locating artful making in a historical context shows us that to become better at artful making, we need to recover an understanding of "ancient making." As we shall see, artful making shares qualities with both ancient and industrial making, drawing on useful aspects of each.

> The metaphor of mass production has become transparent to us, so familiar that we can hardly conceive of anyone having no idea of interchangeable parts, of the potential for increasing value by economies of scale, of the possibilities for efficiently rationalizing the smallest gestures of productive work.

ANCIENT MAKING

Ideas based in Industrial Revolution thinking have become so pervasive in our culture that it's difficult for us to envision what the world was like before they took hold. The controlling metaphor of mass production has become transparent to us, so familiar that we can hardly conceive of anyone having no idea of interchangeable parts, of the potential for increasing value by economies of scale, of the possibilities for efficiently rationalizing—even optimizing—the smallest gestures of productive work. Imagine having none of these ideas available to you. Imagine worrying about making *too much* profit rather than not enough.

To help you cast your thoughts back to a time before the Industrial Revolution, we've invented from many sources a brief composite description of medieval manufacturing. While this manufactory and its owner/operator are not historically factual, the story conforms to the facts of medieval life as scholars have discovered them.[1] In this account, we've tried to represent not only differences from today in ways of working, but also differences in how people doing work might have thought about what they were doing, and in the institutions that influenced their lives.

AN ARMORY ON THE RIVER SEVERN

Hugh of Llangyth, operator of the armor-making foundry in the village of Upton on the banks of the River Severn, has worked ever since he can remember. He knows that to be human is to work, that in work lies salvation and the possibility of a return to the Garden of Eden, to the bliss of God's grace. Sold into apprenticeship by parents who couldn't feed all three children, he went at age nine to Garth, the miller at Upton-upon-Severn. He showed early promise as a fabricator in wood and metal, especially at carving the oaken gears through which the prime mover (the water wheel) drives the great millstones. Since these gears wear out quickly, a good carver is always in demand.

Garth gave his mill to the monks and passed Hugh on to childless Philip the Armorer for a tidy sum. Hugh worked for Philip, first as an apprentice, then as a journeyman, and finally as a master, partner, and almost son. Upon Philip's untimely death (the great wheel took his arm), Hugh, age 19, married Philip's widow, age 30, and began the manufactory's specialization in armor.

He became an important member of the Guild of Heaumers (helmet makers). When that group expanded to form the Armourer's Company, Hugh led the delegation that successfully petitioned the king for a royal charter. He became the area's leading fabricator of arms and armor.

The manufactory has expanded under Hugh's leadership and now includes, in accordance with strict Company rules, two journeymen and four apprentices. He has added, with a dispensation from the Company, half a dozen other skilled workers, under the pressure of his contract with the king for large quantities of munition armor. But the Company has been adamant about restricting Hugh to one shop and one forge; this limit has forced him to send out (for others to make) some of the more complex and delicate parts of the armor: hinges, straps, buckles, actons, etc. The munition armor contract has exacerbated Hugh's usual difficulties in securing supplies of wood, charcoal, and iron. The forest continually retreats before the woodcutters, and flooding in the mines renders them unworkable.

> Johan wants to make a series of anvils, each formed to a stage in the shaping of the armor, and put a man to work on each, so that an armor piece might be handed down a long bench from one man to the next, arriving fully shaped at the end, ready for final assembly.

Hugh cannot approve of the expansions made necessary by large orders for munition armor. He doesn't mind someone other than himself, maybe a journeyman or even a gifted apprentice, working on rings, interlocking and riveting them into a cloth of mail. He tolerates the millman, because he's very good at the dangerous work of polishing the finished plates and because it was this job that killed Philip. He accepts the hammer men, because that is, after all, mere toil, not real work, hammering billets into sheets of varying thickness. But lately, Johan, a young man with an uncanny gift for tempering, that metal mystery no one fully understands, has been pestering him. Johan, who any day now will become a master like Hugh, wants to make a series of anvils, each formed to a stage in the shaping of the armor, and put a man to work on each, so that an armor piece (breastplate, colletin, manifer) might be handed down a long bench from one man to the next, arriving fully shaped at the end, ready for final tempering, polishing, and assembly. Hugh himself, of course, would continue to fit a custom harness to its buyer. But the munition armor could be made without his special attention.

These new methods worry Hugh. A beautiful and effective (for Hugh, the two are the same) harness not only fits like a skin, it grows like a skin in the making as Hugh shapes each tiniest part into interdependent harmony with every other. A harness of armor is part of the man who made it, and the man who made it is a part of the harness. To divide up the making in Johan's way removes something. Hugh doesn't know what to call that something, but he feels the loss keenly. To make one small piece of the whole job, is that man a true Guildsman? Is that work part of the mystery? Or is it mere undignified toil, fit only for unskilled, interchangeable louts performing unskilled, interchangeable gestures?

In his conversations over a stoup of ale at the Pig and Pie with Brother Jerome, whose monastery took over Garth's mill and now has the best collection of river-driven machinery in the valley, Hugh has begun to feel a pressure to embrace something Jerome calls "progress." Brother Jerome has a wide mind for ideas, and he's not always in favor with his abbot. "There should be no limit to our desire to serve well," says Jerome, "for if we have virtue, surely it's the gift of our Blessed Lord, and to fail our gifts is to fail Him." Hugh doesn't buy this; it's too radical.

And yet, what is he to do? How can he personally fabricate and test 1,200 complete harnesses in the time allowed? He can't. It's that simple. How can he refuse such an honor from the king, perhaps letting that idiot over Camberwell way get the commission? He can't. It's that simple.

Sometimes Hugh longs for the good old days, when he worked alone at the forge with only an apprentice to look after the fire. He hammered the plates out of billets he carried himself from the nearby mine. He shaped the plates into the various pieces, each of proper thickness, annealing them to keep them malleable under his hammers. He assembled, took apart, and reassembled the harness over and over, to be sure every piece worked flawlessly with every other, closing the gaps and easing the frictions. He baked the separate parts with charcoal to turn them into steel, then tempered each to just the right combination of hardness and flexibility. And finally, acting as his own millman, he polished each black and rough-edged piece to a smooth, glowing luster, sitting at the great wheel, watching the scale shed off to reveal the gentle colors of the temper, seeing the heart of the metal shine through. Then the oh, so careful final assembly: filing, riveting, buffing, and fitting. Once he made an entire parade armor out of gilt copper instead of steel: a gorgeous, delicate, living thing that fit its man like metal skin, dazzling with its elaborate engravery, red velvet picadills edged in gold, and lobster-tail *chapel de fer*.

The more he ponders, the more this munition armor, ordered in such large numbers, worries Hugh. He makes these harnesses not to measure for a particular man, but to measurements-in-general. They'll be handed out at random to bowmen and pikemen. Hugh knows it's not right. But who can resist the king?

None of that now, alas.

When this commission is filled, he thinks he can go back, perhaps, to his true craft, and ignore Johan's troubling suggestions.

The more he ponders, the more this munition armor, ordered in such large numbers, worries Hugh. He makes these hundreds of harnesses, not to measure for a particular man, but to measurements-in-general. They'll be handed out at random to bowmen and pikemen. This is neither aesthetically or ethically right. The Company knows it's not right; Hugh knows it's not right. But who can resist the king?

Armor should be fitted, and should fit. Hugh hates to think of those 1,200 soldiers, chafing in ill-fitting breastplates and helmets, cursing him for their pain and trouble. Furthermore, these new methods of dividing up the work don't permit the kind of control Hugh needs to guarantee his product honestly. The city inspectors can't keep up with Hugh's production, and this armor goes out with rudimentary inspection, and no view mark at all.

What, after all, are the virtues of good armor? There are two: First, to protect the wearer from the weapons of war. Armor of proof must be tested and warranted against bolt and blow. This cannot be done for so many units. And yet everyone knows the variable quality of ore, iron, and steel. Second, armor must allow the wearer to move freely on horseback and on foot. It can be seen that these virtues are, finally, mutually exclusive: the more protection the armor affords, the heavier and more difficult it is to move around in. That parade armor of copper moved like silk; the baron could dance in it and did, but his woman dented it with her fist when he stepped on her foot. It would never withstand the weakest blow.

One of the armorer's chief mysteries consists of bringing these contrasting virtues together. The armory churns out munition armor so fast that in his heart, Hugh doesn't feel he owns it at all. But he knows who'll be blamed if a bolt pierces a cuirass or a morning star crushes a helmet.

And think: 1,200 complete harnesses, at 16 shillings apiece, with more to come if these are done well. Which they will be; there Hugh can't help himself. He will make them to the best of his ability, and his best is *the* best. But, it is a mixed blessing: What can he do with so many shillings? As Brother Jerome reminds him, God gave him the gift of his skill so that he could keep his family and support his soul, not so that he can pile up the world's goods in this vain way. The worldly reasons for working are as clear in Hugh's mind as the spiritual. Work provides the necessities of life for his body, which in turn supports the life of his soul, and provides some cushion against the vagaries of climate and conditions. It prevents idleness, the source of so many evils; it restrains concupiscence by mortifying the flesh; and it allows him to give alms. But, 1,200 harnesses—that's a lot of alms.

It's hard to think about; makes Hugh's head hurt. Brother Jerome puts it into words so easily, with four main questions:

- How can the Armourer's Company maintain its standards of quality in the face of the demand for quantity?
- To what degree must munition armor be of the same quality as the custom-made harness designed and built for a particular man?

■ At what point does a harness made in Hugh's manufactory cease to be the product of his work, and become an impersonal object, no part of God's purpose? At what point does the work become mere toil, no contribution to God's glory or Hugh's salvation?

■ Finally, to what degree must the craft guild care? If the armor protects, isn't that enough?

THE COSTS AND BENEFITS OF ANCIENT MAKING

About making goods for sale, Hugh of Llangyth and others like him had complex sensibilities different from ours. The ancient fabricator made unique things one at a time. While the basic form and purpose of a given product might remain constant (what started out to be a wheel ended up a wheel), the ancient fabricator understood that everything in that wheel, including his work, depended on everything else.

A maker (say, a wheelwright) performed operations on materials (wood, metal) and arranged them in a form, for a purpose. A wheel has two forms: (1) the ideal—perfectly round; and (2) the actual—as round as possible given the materials and the maker's skill. Each wheel fills many functions, has many purposes, depending on your point of view. A pair of wheels carries a cart, a major purpose; at the same time, making and selling them provides a living for the wheelwright. For the farmer who hauls his produce to market, they also provide a living.

The main problem with Hugh's way of working, as viewed from our modern perspective, is that his making process was very expensive. In Hugh's armory, the costs we identified in Chapter 4—reconfiguration and exploration costs—tended to be high, and he incurred them every time he made any thing. Much of the time and effort he devoted to assuring that a breastplate would be just the right size and shape for the particular individual who would wear it, we would now call a reconfiguration cost. Most of his materials resisted reconfiguration. To change iron ore into steel, and to shape steel into parts of a harness of armor, was difficult and time-consuming. Because he worked with expensive, often rare materials, Hugh incurred high exploration costs nearly every time he tried something new, which he did in some small way at least every time he made something for a unique person.

Hugh did not think in these terms, of course. He aimed to make a thing that fitted its purpose as well as his art and craft would permit. He had no alternative, therefore, but to incur constant reconfiguration and exploration costs. Changing to fit the purpose and exploring the best ways to do that were fundamental parts of his work on each thing he made, the most important part of what he was doing. Because these activities cost a lot, he charged a high price. It's no coincidence that his primary customer was the king. Most ordinary men could not afford Hugh's armor. Commissions for armor were few, limited by the population of rich men. The limits on transactions that could occur meant, in modern terms, relatively little value creation. Replicated across the society, such limited value creation supported a dismal standard of living.

Figure 5–1 illustrates the nature of transactions in Hugh's armory. Because Hugh incurs the high costs associated with reconfiguration and exploration nearly every time he makes something, it doesn't matter much, in terms of average cost, how many he makes. His process is customized to its purpose, and so making requires the same magnitude of expenditure each time he does it. We see this in Figure 5–1, in the shape of the "Ancient Making Cost" curve, which is relatively flat. Whether Hugh makes one unit or 100, the cost of making each one is pretty constant.

The benefit provided to the customer is a different story, though. Hugh makes everything one at a time and one of a kind. In modern terms, he customizes his product to the needs of a particular buyer. This means that the product provides considerable value to the person for whom it is intended, and not nearly as much to someone else. The benefit from Hugh's way of working, therefore, is much greater for the first unit he makes than for subsequent units of the same thing. Actually, Hugh would not ordinarily think of making a second unit

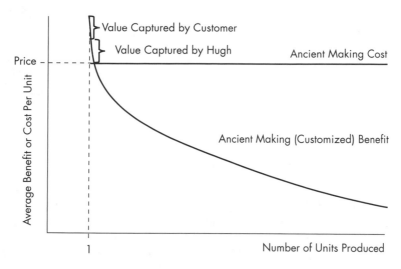

FIGURE 5-1
The benefits and costs of ancient making.

exactly like the first (unless the customer ordered multiples for himself), because that's not the way he works. In Figure 5–1, we see then that the benefit of a made things falls off dramatically after the first unit is made, reflecting the fact that a second unit is not valuable to someone for whom it is not customized. The second unit of armor, made for a tall nobleman, will poorly fit the next short nobleman who walks into Hugh's shop—most of the time anyway.

We can see also from Figure 5–1 that this way of working—customizing every made thing—yields one transaction, for one unit. The customer pays a price somewhere between the benefit for that unit and its cost, and each party to the transaction captures value. Hugh gets paid more than it costs him to make the armor; the customer gets a benefit that is worth more than the price he paid. Even if Hugh were inclined to make another unit just like this one, he would have to sell it at a loss. The customized item is not valuable enough to someone else (someone other than the person for whom it was customized) to command a price higher than the cost of making it. Hence, value creation and value capture through buying and selling proceed slowly in this ancient world.

Toward Industrial Making

Some version of Hugh's manufactory could have been running in England or on the continent anywhere from 900–1500. The earlier we imagine Hugh's foundry, the more heartfelt the connection between a maker and his product. His idea that the harness would grow under his making, its many parts fitting each to the other, persisted throughout this time, but gradually the idea of interdependence among the maker, materials, form, and purpose wore away.

As the world grew more commercial, the armor's final purpose, its cause for being, evolved from fulfilling the vocation of the maker (to do God's work) and a function for the buyer (to protect him from bolts and blows) to include increasing profit for the maker and eventually for a seller, a person in

As the world grew more commercial, the mystery moved from making to figuring out how to make.

the middle who had nothing to do with the making or the wearing. As earlier purposes became part of new commercial ones, relationships among maker, materials, and form gradually changed from organic interdependence to a carefully preplanned and rigidly systematic arrangement. The mystery moved from *making* to *figuring out how to make*. The sensibility of a maker developed toward modern times, moving from that of Master Hugh to that of young Johan, and eventually to Eli Whitney, Henry Ford, and Frederick Taylor.

Industrial Making

We can bring our historical context up to date through the ideas, familiar in one way or another to most of us, of three major historical figures:

- Eli Whitney conceived of a made thing as assembled of interchangeable parts.
- Henry Ford exploited Whitney's conception and added to it a continuously moving assembly line, proving that economies of scale could drive down unit cost and allow

price reductions that increased sales and thereby increased profits.

■ Frederick Winslow Taylor developed revolutionary tool steels that made past shop practice obsolete, then replaced craft guild experience with standardized work practices.

Most modern thought about making uses categories derived from the work of these men and those who came after them.

ELI WHITNEY

Whitney never profited as he expected to from his most memorable invention, the cotton gin; patent disputes and outright theft tied it up in litigation for most of his life. He did, however, achieve a national reputation as a master maker of machines. In this *persona*, he boldly offered the Secretary of the Treasury a proposition that "announced," as his biographer put it, ". . . the advent of America's industrial future."[2] Whitney offered to "undertake to Manufacture ten or Fifteen Thousand Stand of Arms."[3] That he had only recently ever seen a musket up-close offered no impediment to his enterprising boldness. He chose to make muskets after deciding that only the national government had the resources he needed to implement his manufacturing ideas. He then asked himself what the government needed that he could make with his as-yet-untried "interchangeable system." The government needed muskets; he decided on muskets. He was thinking in a way that Hugh could not have: about how to structure his new factory *before* he decided what to make in it.

Having made his choice and sold his plan, Whitney acquired a pair of muskets to copy. He analyzed the weapon into its parts and designed a machine to make each part. Whitney's methods achieved unprecedented levels of accuracy in dimensions and shape. No human machinist with his drills and files could approach the machine for speed, consistency, and tirelessness. Parts made so accurately could be swapped among muskets. For a meeting in the nation's capitol, Whitney piled a supply of his musket parts onto a big conference table and invited officials to build a working musket right there, taking parts at random from his piles. They did it easily.[4] This feature made assembly in the factory much quicker and caused a great leap in ease of field repairs that in turn resulted in an enormous step up in quality throughout the industry. No one would buy a musket not made to these tolerances. And, of course, these advances attracted makers of all kinds of other things.

Whitney was thinking in a way that Hugh could not have: about how to structure his new factory before he decided what to make in it.

HENRY FORD

As a child in the 1880s, Ford dreamed about manufacturing watches. He just knew he could "build a good serviceable watch for around thirty cents." He calculated his breakeven point at 2,000 watches per day. "Even then," he went on to say, "I wanted to make something in quantity."[5] A little over 35 years later, he'd be thinking about Model T Ford automobiles, and about bringing the price below $500, to a point where his own workers could buy one. For the year 1916–17, his Highland Park factory would turn out over 2,000 cars per day.

This way of organizing work became known as "mass production." The ideas of mass production, the interchangeable system, and efficient assembly were in the air of the new century. Most of the elements of Ford's Highland Park factory were in use somewhere in manufacturing; Ford and his men both borrowed and invented as they gradually reduced the time it took to make a car, and thus lower its price. At most automobile factories, men carried the chassis from station to station until it got wheels. Then they pushed it. Under Ford's personal direction a remarkable group of engineers and shop foremen created a *system* of conveyors and *moving* assembly lines that brought needed parts and the accumulating chassis together at just the right times and places.

In the spring of 1913, James Purdy, in charge of magneto assembly, introduced the first moving assembly line to Ford's factory. Before Purdy made his changes, one man, standing at a counter, assembled each magneto out of parts from nearby bins. Average assembly time was about 20 minutes. Purdy divided the job into 29 operations performed by 29 men as the magnetos passed in front of them on a continuously moving belt. This arrangement cut assembly time to an average of 13 minutes and 10 seconds. When, some months later, the belt was moved up off the floor so the men no longer had to stoop to pick up and replace the magnetos, the time dropped further to seven minutes. Further study of individual operations brought the time down to five minutes. As soon as Ford could sell enough cars to need this many magnetos, a savings in time of 75% resulted, each man on the line producing as much as four men had before.

The idea of continuously moving lines spread throughout the factory. Engine assembly came next, then transmissions, then the whole car itself. According to Ford biographer Allan Nevins, in August 1913, it took 12.5 man-hours to assemble a chassis. The first crude experimental moving assembly line cut that time to 5 hours, 50 minutes. On December 1, 1913, the time fell to 2 hours, 38 minutes; and by January 1914, it had fallen to an average of 1 hour, 33 minutes.[6] The fastest time recorded for assembling a stationary chassis had been 728 minutes, just under 12.5 hours. In less than a year, assembly time had been reduced by a factor of eight. The number of cars produced increased amazingly: in 1911–12, the company made 78,440 Model Ts; 168,304 in 1912–13; 248,307 in 1913–14; and in 1916–17, an astonishing 730,041.[7]

FREDERICK WINSLOW TAYLOR[8]

Taylor focused the ideas Whitney and Ford used for parts and chassis and applied them to the workers themselves. What, he wanted to know, could a particular tool, a particular machine, and a particular worker accomplish in a day if they worked together at peak efficiency? Before Taylor, the answer to this and related questions lay in the accumulated shop wisdom of the workers. Hugh and his fellow armorers banded together in a guild to protect their mysteries,

> Taylor saw his mission clearly: to pry open the workers' mysteries—expose them to the light of day, of calculation, of "science"—and so make life better for everyone.

evolved over the centuries and ceremoniously handed down from master to apprentice. Taylor saw his mission clearly: to pry open those mysteries—expose them to the light of day, of calculation, of "science"—and so make life better for everyone, especially the workers.

This desire to improve not only the owner's profits but the worker's situation led him to make sure that, when he set the rates and quotas for a day's work, he had based his numbers on quantities objectively measured. To establish such rational values, he broke jobs down into their smallest gestures. Positioned at the machinist's shoulder, he tirelessly timed every move over and over, suggesting improvements in arrangements and even individual gestures, until he could honestly present his rate, method, and quota as the best way to do the best possible job with the least wasted effort.

This led him to experiment with pay rates. How much money would it take to assuage a worker for the loss of personal autonomy and authority over the work? What, in other words, would it cost to keep the worker at it when the work itself had lost most of its former appeal? As it naturally did when a clean-handed clerk took over the shop floor and wrote down the job on an instruction card, a clerk who probably couldn't actually do the work. By doing the job exactly according to Taylor's instruction card, a worker could increase, even double, the day's pay. By failing to do the job exactly as ordered, a worker could reduce the day's pay alarmingly. Taylor wanted no individual initiative. He applied Whitney's idea of interchangeable parts to the workers in the shop; they became units of labor, easily moved from job to job.

In the drive to quantify machine-shop work, Taylor and metallurgist Maunsel White conducted an extensive series of tests measuring and recording the speeds at which various tools could cut steel. In this process, they heated some tools well beyond temperatures "known" to ruin tool steel. To everyone's astonishment, the ruined steel cut faster and wore longer than any of the traditionally tempered tools, by a factor of four or five. They took out patents, and in the summer of 1900 Bethlehem Steel mounted an exhibit at the Paris

Exposition. Although placed far from the center of the exposition's activities, the Bethlehem lathe, cutting steel at unheard-of speeds, churning out chips blue with heat from which you could light a cigarette, stole the show.

The historically most important consequences of Taylor-White steel were not visible in the sensational demonstrations at the 1900 Paris Exposition. The new cutting tools rendered the mysteries of the past, the worker's advantage, obsolete. None of the craft wisdom passed along the centuries from master to apprentice applied to these new steels. This meant that Taylor had a free hand to apply his analytic systems everywhere in the shop.

Just as Whitney broke his musket down into its basic parts, Taylor analyzed each step of a job into its smallest coherent gestures. Most jobs, he found, were made up of the same old gestures, differently arranged. These basic parts of a job could be organized each time a new job came into the shop, and this organizing could be done, not by the machinist according to outmoded wisdom and personal convenience, but by a new worker, the creation of Taylor's genius, the *rate clerk*, with an expertise in rates and numbers, not machinery. With clean hands and a white collar, in an office far from the clamor of machines, tools, and other workers, the rate clerk could list the gestures required for any job, sum up the time they should take according to Taylor's research, and deliver an instruction card (carefully wrapped to protect it from the machinist's dirty hands) telling a worker exactly how to do the job and how much time to take doing it. Control of the shop, of making itself, passed from the machinist skilled in metal working to the clerk skilled in number crunching. With the essential expertise resident in the rate clerk, the firm could hire fewer skilled and more inexperienced workers—less skilled, less experienced, less expensive.

THE EVOLUTION OF SEQUENTIAL PROCESSES

As manufacturers improved their shop methods, those methods took on a new shape. To achieve interchangeability of musket parts, to create the productivity gains of the Highland Park factory, every single part of every product had to be painstakingly, and completely specified in advance. Taylor's rate clerks similarly pre-specified every aspect of the process of making parts and products. Design activities became separate from production activities. The people responsible for advance specification of parts and processes took up residence in separate areas of the factory and eventually left for separate white-collar buildings.

To achieve interchangeability of parts, every part had to be painstakingly specified in advance. Taylor's rate clerks pre-specified every aspect of the process of making. Design activities became separate from production activities. The people responsible for advance specification of parts and processes took up residence in separate areas of the factory and eventually left for separate white-collar buildings.

By applying technology and reorganizing work in this way, industrial makers could drive down unit costs and allow more transactions to occur. Workers—ordinary men and women—would be able to buy things that formerly only the rich could afford. Henry Ford understood this very well:

> . . . in making the price on the four-cylinder runabout, the question was not, "How much can we get for this car?" but "How low can we sell it and still make a small margin on each one? How many cars must be turned out to get the lowest cost per car, and will the demand absorb this tremendous output?"[9]

Here we can see the singular brilliance of the changes we described in our brief evocations of Whitney, Ford, and Taylor. We can express the logic of their advances this way: If high costs of reconfiguration and exploration limit our ability to transact, *let's stop incurring these costs in production.* How? *We can stop adjusting each thing to its unique purpose. Let the customer adjust.*

Like many great ideas, this one is simple, obvious in hindsight, and radically subversive in its time. Of course, industrial methods don't avoid the costs of reconfiguration and exploration, but only extract them from making itself, and place them at the front end of the process, transforming them into what we now call "product development" and "process engineering." The costs associated with reconfiguration and exploration in these early stages of a sequential process can then be shared by a large number of units emerging from a standardized manufacturing process. The average cost of making one unit of the made thing is significantly reduced. The great leap here was the insight that *if costs can be lowered enough, customers won't mind that the product no longer perfectly suits them*. Many customers will happily buy a knife that, although not perfectly suited to them, cuts pretty well, provided its price is low enough. They will trade unique perfection for affordability and availability.

With costs thus lowered for many common items, many more transactions become possible. People who previously could have only one knife in their household can suddenly afford several. This creates new value, for the seller in the form of profit not there before, and for the buyer in the form of useful (if not perfect) knives that before cost too much. Every one of these new transactions creates additional value, additional wealth. And as the descendants of Whitney, Ford, and Taylor continued to refine production systems, the world benefited from more transactions that created ever more value. Thus, the great economic engine that supports the standard of living of the developed world came into being.

When Henry Ford made Model Ts, he incurred reconfiguration and exploration costs in advance, before most units were produced. When he made 10,000 units, he reduced the per-unit reconfiguration and exploration costs by a factor of 10,000, radically bringing down the average cost of making each car. With his up-front costs thus diffused, he could price a car much, much lower than if he used Hugh's methods. Many more transactions could occur, because many more people were willing to accept a mass-produced car they could afford, rather than paying what a specially crafted car would cost, or doing without.

Figure 5–2 depicts the arrangements of benefits and costs in Ford's way of making. The sequential structure of the process, which allows reconfiguration and exploration costs to be spread across a large number of units, yields economies of scale. If we produce a large number of similar units, the average cost to make each unit drops, dramatically. In Figure 5–2, the "Industrial Making Cost" curve is not flat, but dips sharply, reflecting this way of reorganizing work. That's a good thing, because when we make products for the average user rather than customizing for each individual, the items we are making provide an average benefit that is lower than the customized benefit. In Figure 5–2, the "Industrial Making Benefit" curve has become flat. If the cost curve dips far enough, though, we can achieve larger numbers of transactions—many transactions, in fact. Getting the cost curve to dip far enough is the point of Ford's and Purdy's cleverness in rearranging the Highland Park factory. Because the costs implicit in customization were high, there was plenty of potential for "industrialization." In Figure 5–2, the distance k represents this potential for industrialization, the limits within which the cleverness of Ford and Purdy can operate freely to create value.

Although Ford might make a smaller profit on each unit using this approach than if he made customized vehicles, he can generate many more transactions by doing it this way, which ends up making much more profit. As the old joke goes (although it is perfectly correct in this case), he doesn't worry about the loss of profit margin because he can "make up for it in volume." Many more transactions mean much more value creation. Value creation happens more rapidly than before. Many

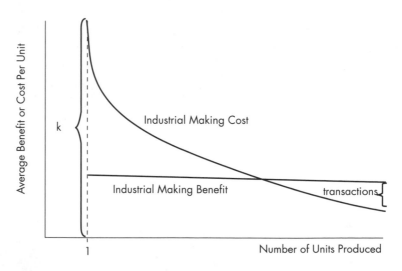

FIGURE 5–2
The benefits and costs of industrial making.

more people can participate in this market, can benefit from these transactions. In a real sense, the region of transactions in Figure 5–2 is the heart of the Industrial Revolution engine, the engine of increase in standards of living across the world.

TOWARD ARTFUL MAKING

As "Taylorism" became more refined, and more widely used in American and European industry, it created an increasingly sharp (and invidious) distinction between knowing and doing, thinking and making, and between classes of workers, white- and blue-collar. The new class, the white collars, formed the backbone of what came to be called "scientific management." Taylor genuinely believed that implementing his principles improved the lot of working men. But that modifier, "working," tells the true story. By distinguishing between "working" and something else, the division of white from blue collars had the effect of dehumanizing the blue collars. The new, scientific managers increasingly conceived of "workers" as material on which they could perform money-saving and profit-increasing operations. In thinking this way, they lost access to the worker's skill, experience, and resourcefulness. As managers embraced and developed Taylor's ideas, they went awry.

ARTFUL MAKING

How does artful making fit into this evolving picture? As we have seen in Chapter 4, a prerequisite for artful making is low cost of iteration. In Figure 5–3, we show how artful making, with its cheap and rapid iteration, enters into our historical context. Low cost of iteration, which derives from low reconfiguration and exploration costs, amounts to a low cost of making the first, unique unit. Knowledge work, which manipulates and transforms ideas, symbols, and other "thought-stuff," can have lower cost of iteration than physical work because it's easier to change thoughtstuff than to re-form metal once it's bent the wrong way. The materials of making are, on

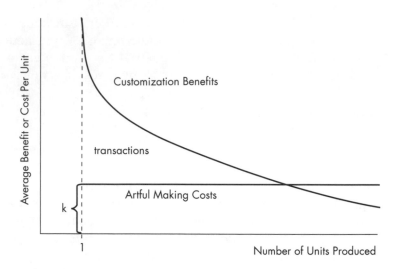

FIGURE 5–3
The benefits and costs of artful making.

average, more "pliable" in knowledge work. Moreover, technology has been applied in many artful making contexts to further lower the costs of reconfiguration and exploration, mostly through the application of IT to allow rapid prototyping, simulation, and other related methods. Systems that allow frequent, inexpensive builds of a software application are examples of this kind of enabling technology.

The result, shown in Figure 5–3, is a low cost of making the first unit. The indicator of potential for industrialization, k, is small. You could arrange work processes in a sequential, industrial manner here, but you wouldn't gain much. The rationale for sequential, industrial arrangement of work has weakened.

But that's not the whole story. Because industrialization offers less potential benefit, the work no longer needs to be directed toward the needs of an average user. We can move back toward customizing, toward making what the customer wants, as we did in ancient making. Hugh would be glad to see that we can again craft a product to its specific purpose. No longer does a customer need to put up with the knowledge work equivalent of a knife that doesn't quite fit the hand. A software program, a strategy, a play production, these can be made in tremendous variety and subtle variations. Structured artfully, the making process can produce outcomes to suit different conditions, companies, and challenges.

Mass production developed out of the need to diffuse high reconfiguration and exploration costs across a large number of units. When those costs are not very high to begin with, we don't need to do this. Instead, we can claim larger margins from individualized transactions, and we can engage in such transactions again and again. We can move from a large number of cheap and rapid *repetitive* transactions, to a large number of cheap and rapid *iterative* transactions. Instead of a large number of similar units, as in industrial settings, we can make an ongoing (in fact, theoretically unending) series of units different from each other, each one benefiting from unique innovations. We can reconceive the outcome each time, thereby achieving a large number of transactions that create value. This way of working moves the creation of value a step beyond industrial methods.

LEARNING TO MAKE ARTFULLY

We can think of many advances in making practices in the last half of the 20th Century as the result of straining backward toward ancient making and forward toward artful making approaches. Quality management guru W. Edwards Deming and others realized that the workers themselves were best positioned to understand the complexities of the evolving systems of making. They saw that in a rapidly changing world the value of customization and innovation would increase. Technology would be applied to drive down the costs of reconfiguring plants and equipment. The game would shift from efficiency to improvement, from replication to innovation. Rate clerks and their modern equivalents, with their clean hands and inexperienced notions of the job, could not be the primary drivers of improvement, of innovation. To improve the system, the workers themselves would have to take the initiative for managing and monitoring the processes under their control, adjusting them as necessary. Workers would once again have to be thought of as people, with individual skills and flaws, not as interchangeable parts. Thinking about workers as people would lead inexorably to considering how to make profitable use of *all* their powers, not just a few mechanical gestures.

In the coming chapters, we will turn to deeper exploration of how companies, business and theatre, extend the idea of reconnecting with the worker's resourcefulness. As we will show in the next chapter, movement toward artful making begins with a revised understanding of "control" in a making process. The idea of control embodied in the rate clerk's laminated instruction card, which requires absolute worker compliance, conflicts with the idea of relying on worker resourcefulness. To achieve the innovation benefits of empowered workers without negating the efficiencies of standardized work practices, we must examine and resolve the quandary of control.

ENDNOTES

1.   Examination of the history of daily life in ancient times is a recent development in scholarship. For obvious reasons (they didn't write about themselves; no one wrote about them), it's hard to find out about ordinary people. See the bibliography for citations of the works we consulted in our invention of Hugh.

2.   Jeannette Mirsky and Allan Nevins, *The World of Eli Whitney* (New York: The MacMillan Company, 1952) p. 137.

3.   Mirsky and Nevins, p. 138.

4.   About 1,000 years after Hugh and 100 years or so after Whitney, a pleasant symmetry occurred when, in 1908, in a test sanctioned and supervised by the Royal Automobile Club of Great Britain, three of Henry Leland's stock Cadillacs were dismantled, their parts thoroughly shuffled, and three new cars assembled, started, and driven away.

5.   Henry Ford, *My Life and Work* (Garden City, NY: Doubleday, 1922) p. 24.

6. Allan Nevins, *Ford: The Times, the Man, the Company*, with the collaboration of Frank Ernest Hill (New York: Charles Scribner and Sons, 1954) p. 471ff.

7. Nevins, p. 475.

8. Sources for this section include Frederick Winslow Taylor, *The Principles of Scientific Management* (New York: W. W. Norton, 1967; first published in 1911 by Frederick W. Taylor); and Robert Kanigel, *The One Best Way: Frederick Taylor and the Enigma of Efficiency* (New York: Viking Penguin, a division of Penguin Books USA, 1997).

9. *Cycle and Automobile Trade Journal*, X (January 1, 1906). Quoted in Nevins, p. 282.

6 ARTFUL MAKING TURNS INDUSTRIAL NOTIONS OF CONTROL UPSIDE DOWN

Artful making strives to realize fully the benefits of workers' talents and skills. It calls on us to recognize individual differences among workers and to acknowledge the importance of group chemistry. It stresses reliance on conversation and other informal modes of interaction over the use of documents and formal mechanisms. It's antithetical to purely analytical approaches that equate people with interchangeable units of labor. Where you find artful making, you find people working on the same tasks together, as rough equals or as apprentices and masters. You find people doing many things in parallel, trying and trying again, iteratively, in a way that may appear unstructured and confused. You find product and service standards, but not standardized work practices. For all these reasons, artful making calls for careful thinking about what it means to manage employees.

MANAGING PEOPLE WHO ARE SMARTER THAN YOU ARE

Lucinda Duncalfe Holt, a software industry consultant and former company CEO, has encountered firsthand the challenges of getting the most out of highly talented software developers who have their own ideas about how work should be done:

They're very difficult to control. This may be the most difficult issue we face. . . .When the chips are down they tend to be . . . your most precious commodity—and your worst nightmare. You have no idea what they're doing. They sit there with 42 little windows open on their 17-inch monitor.[1]

Ivan Sutherland, one of the leaders in the early efforts to build the Internet, notes of highly skilled individuals that, "You can maybe convince them that something's of interest and importance, but you cannot tell them what to do."[2] Similarly, Abigail Adams observes of her role with respect to the actors that she is "not on the journey with them." When you ask talented people to explore, you, as a director/manager, usually cannot go everywhere they can. This is partly because of skill differences. Great directors are not necessarily great actors; great project managers are not necessarily great designers, engineers, or programmers. You don't need all the specialized talents and skills of your employees to lead the group effectively. It would be wildly impractical to try to maintain those skills *and* to manage at the same time. But just as clearly, not knowing all of what your employees are doing, not being able to see all the possibilities that they can see, complicates notions of control. How does a great director/manager achieve control? What does "control" even mean in this context?

SUPERVISION IN AN INDUSTRIAL CONTEXT

Answering these questions was easier in earlier times, in Frederick Taylor's world, for example. There control meant, quite simply, getting workers to do what you wanted them to do, often to comply with carefully designed work specifications (instruction cards). What you did to accomplish this you called "supervision." In the simplest cases, supervision meant keeping an eye on things, looking over workers' shoulders. When you couldn't watch workers

When you ask talented people to explore, you, as a director/manager, usually cannot go everywhere they can.

closely, you could rely on *compliance mechanisms*, administrative techniques designed to make workers *want* to comply with work specifications.

Tell them what to do; fire them if they don't do it. That's one brand of compliance mechanism. Although crude, this sort of mechanism has a long history and isn't hard to find in use today.[3] Compliance mechanisms can be more complex and subtle, though. They can be based on reward rather than threat, directly as in commission systems that pay more when a performance metric increases, or indirectly, as in promises: "You will be promoted to sales manager if you increase your sales by 50%." The idea, always, is to design a reason for workers to want to do what managers need.

MANAGEMENT IN AN ARTFUL CONTEXT

Holt comes from a family of artists. She understands that things get much more complicated when you're dealing with knowledge workers. Speaking of difficult-to-manage, impossible-to-supervise groups of technical wizards, she notes:

> When [your business shifts] you'll often find the seed for the shift in that group because they're not really paying attention to you all along anyway. They were worried about some way-out-there trend. They'll see it and there will be something there. [The key to managing] change is in that group of folks you don't have a lot of control over.[4]

Not only can you not understand what your wizards are doing—who is doing what, who caused what problem, etc.—but your compliance mechanisms themselves become a problem because they keep workers doing what they're doing even when what they *ought* to be doing changes. Holt suggests that there's a big upside in having specially skilled and talented workers who are "out of control." Computer industry consultant and author Tom DeMarco, speaking about software development projects, makes a similar point:

> The best thing you can do on a project is get on top of an absolutely out-of-control team that's headed in the right direction. . . .you can't steer it, you can't make it go faster or slower, but it is making tremendous progress.[5]

Compliance mechanisms, no matter how cleverly designed, inhibit exploration of paths that managers cannot anticipate. True instruments of industrial making, they presume that whatever needs to be done can be anticipated, that you *can* and *do* know where you are going before you start out on every journey. David Bradley, a People's Light director, extends these ideas to explain his view of the differences between directing and conventional supervision:

> My friends and family who don't do theatre are astounded when they find out the director is not at every performance. From a "management" standpoint, they can't believe I'm not backstage making sure they're doing it exactly the same way, or fixing it. . . Performance is different than making sure that a Toyota looks the same each time it gets made. If actors and directors tried to make every performance the same, sooner or later the performance would be awful. If I sit and watch each time and tell an actor, "You did the line a little differently tonight," then the actor's trying to say the line a certain way, as opposed to being alive in the moment. . . It's not about what the director did. I don't perform.[6]

A common thread runs through the thoughts of Holt, Sutherland, Adams, DeMarco, and Bradley: Forcing workers to comply with preconceptions often hinders the overall making process.

SOME NEW REALITIES OF MANAGEMENT

We watched this idea play out in the story of how Sun Microsystems embraced the Web. The techies who saw the really important "way-out-there" trend defied their superiors (at one noisy meeting it almost came to mutiny), and the company was better off in the end because of it. Sun's employees reacted vehemently to the industrial compliance mechanism of a $50 monthly charge for using the Web, in part because they sensed the violence that such a mechanism would do to their ethos of exploration.

Compliance mechanisms inhibit exploration of paths that managers themselves cannot anticipate. True instruments of industrial making, they presume what needs to be done *can* be anticipated, that you *can* and *do* know where you are going before you start every journey.

For an increasing percentage of 21st Century work, the supervisory equation has changed. According to historical wisdom, supervisors: (1) encourage sound practice and habits, and (2) encourage changes in practice and habits as changing conditions require. Managers, increasingly different from supervisors, cannot accept these principles. For them, following their employees as often as leading them, the equation must read: (1) encourage sound practices and habits, and (2) encourage employees to push for changes in practices and habits when they see conditions changing. Sun's bottom-up control exactly suits the task of managing control-aversive, individualistic talent, aiming at a moving target.

In business, when we talk about "control" we usually mean some kind of restraint. This finds its way into the theatre also. Young actors hear very early in their careers this story, told about George Abbott, a legendary Broadway director who meticulously planned and micro-managed his productions, who knew in advance exactly what he wanted from everyone:

> Suddenly, in the middle of the scene, Abbot interrupted a young actor: "When you say that line, please move down left." The actor, flustered by the break in his concentration, walked to the edge of the stage and looked at Abbot: "What's my motivation?" he asked. Long pause. Then, quietly but with absolute finality, Abbot said: "Your job."

Abbot produced popular work despite this technique, and there are other examples of directors like this. There are always exceptions, people who make things work through unique feats of personal genius. But absent a genius, for reliable innovation we need a different kind of control.

CONTROL IN ARTFUL MAKING

We've been discussing a shift from supervision to management, a shift away from the restraint of compliance mechanisms toward—what? Certainly we don't advocate an "anything goes" style of management. We aren't talking about giving up all influence over workers. Adams's emergent style of directing includes the presumption that she will exercise considerable influence over the making and the ultimate product. She retains a position of authority in the ensemble, whether she uses it conventionally or not. Just as clearly, we don't envision a supervisor patrolling the workspace, cracking a whip and barking out orders. So, how *do* we define control in artful making?

We offer a deeply counterintuitive answer to this question. Control through *release* sounds like no control at all. So goes the sentiment of executives inclined to criticize Sun's management in HBS' executive education classes. But remember, control through release makes it possible for a play at People's Light to finish within 30 seconds of its over two-hour running time, every time. Artful making can produce finely controlled outcomes, but not by imposing compliance mechanisms on the workers.

> Control through *release* sounds like no control at all. But control through release makes it possible for a play at People's Light to finish within 30 seconds of exactly the same time every night.

The first and most basic quality of artful work is Release. Without Release, nothing else happens. It's the foundation on which we build the other artful making qualities (Collaboration, Ensemble, and Play). Although Release is a general and widely applicable concept, it is easiest to see and understand in its physical form, as it affects individuals. It is here, with individuals working to achieve physical outcomes, that we begin explaining this nonindustrial notion of control.

PHYSICAL RELEASE

The pitcher takes a big breath and whooshes it out before going into his windup. He throws without thinking too much, free of psychological micro-management. We say he has his "good stuff," he has his "control." When he gets frightened or otherwise distracted, he loses confidence in what he calls his "mechanics," those gestures he has practiced countless times until he can do them without conscious thought. He no longer believes that if he just lets it go the ball will arrive where it should. He tenses up, loses his stuff, and starts aiming the ball, and walking batters.

Watch a golfer address the ball. A simple but by no means easy sport, golf requires exquisite control and a perfect lack of tension. Sergio García, a famous "waggler," spends as much as half a minute on the tee, settling, making sure no tension remains before he unleashes the prodigious effort of the drive. At the 2002 U.S. Open, the *New York Times* reported that García averaged 23 pre-swing waggles during its informal (three-hole) survey.[7] Everything a golfer does requires delicate control of movements that must be free of any restraint. The physics of the game are evident to anyone (ball goes where clubface directs it), but getting the mechanics right has made strong men and women cry.

Actors present clear examples of Release, and its opposite, *restraint*. If you get a chance, notice the difference between Candice Bergen (television's *Murphy Brown*, 1988, also recently in *Miss Congeniality*, 2000), an actor who works from tension, and, say, Meryl Streep (*River Wild*, 1994) or John Malkovich (*Dangerous Liaisons*, 1988). Look at Bergen's straining, corded neck. Then watch Streep's uncanny physical calm at the oars of a bouncing raft hurtling down river rapids. Or watch the first few moments of *Dangerous Liaisons* as Malkovich walks along a palace hallway in his finery.

The way people walk displays many of the tensions they carry with them all the time. Watch someone walk and you can see how they hold tension in certain parts of their bodies. Look at their shoulders. See how their hands swing asymmetrically at the ends of their arms. Observe the difference in how people walk ordinarily and how they walk when they know you're watching. Ask a friend to watch you walk and feel the tensions in your own body. Remember the first time you gave a presentation at a meeting? Those horrifying moments when you stood up and walked to the front of the room, everyone's attention on you, how your arms and legs suddenly belonged to someone else, how they wouldn't follow your instructions? That's physical tension.

A costume designer once told Lee that when singer Kathryn Grayson was making historical romance movies, her boned strapless gowns needed elastic gussets at the sides of her waist to accommodate eight inches of expansion when she took a breath to sing. Eight inches! That's physical release.

Actors release to gain power and to increase the flexibility of their physical instrument. Their process is similar to that of athletes, but instead of throwing a ball or swinging a club, an actor walks, eats, speaks, laughs, or cries. These are everyday activities; we all do them all the time, but not in the difficult conditions of play making. Actors need to practice, just as athletes, singers, and painters do. But instead of practicing a dedicated movement, like a golf swing, they practice dozens of moves. In their practice, they encounter and also strive to master a more general version of release, called "mind release," which is highly relevant to the art of innovation in business.

MIND RELEASE AND FOCUS

The mental equivalent of physical tension is inhibition. We require inhibitions to get along in the world, but they can interfere with some things we want to do. The ordinarily useful inhibition against making a fool of yourself can interfere with making the outrageous suggestion that electrifies the meeting; in severe form, inhibition can keep you from having outrageous thoughts to begin with. Actors cultivate mind release from these inhibitions to gain access to deep feelings or outrageous ideas; when they do gain access, they need further release to give themselves permission to express those feelings and ideas in public. Knowledge workers must learn to do the same, not so much with feelings, but with ideas.

To achieve (and then make use of) Release requires *focus*, skill at directing attention away from a source of tension. The pitcher cannot let himself concentrate too hard on that tying run in scoring position. Sergio García must vanquish his obsession with that ball-eating water hazard he's already visited for a bogie five. The problem is that you can't simply instruct your mind not to think about an unhelpful thing. That doesn't work. To avoid a particular thought, you must put something else in its place. You cannot, that is, stand in a corner and *not* think of a white elephant. You can, with practice (lots of practice), learn to stand in a corner and think of a gray elephant instead. The best way to understand this concept of focus is to experience it. Here's a brief exercise that can help you understand focus while you're sitting in your chair:

Focus is the primary means by which the director influences efforts at release. A director/manager cannot necessarily know what workers are doing; he/she cannot tell them what to do. But often, he/she can influence focus.

Position yourself as comfortably as possible. When you're set, take a quick mental tour around yourself to see if you're tense anywhere. Do your best to relax. Close your eyes. Focus your attention on breathing, just on your breathing: in, and out; in, and out. Slow your breath down a little so that your breathing is conscious, not automatic. Now, begin counting your breaths. When you reach four, start over. Focus your attention on your breathing alone, nothing else.

You'll find yourself thinking all over the place. That's okay, though, because that gets you to the heart of the exercise. Every time you notice yourself thinking about something besides breathing, *stop to acknowledge what you're thinking about*. Do it in silent talk to yourself, in words. And then, deliberately, with silent language, put your focus back on breathing. Returning your focus is the heart of the exercise. If you are like most people, the exercise will go something like this:

Breathing, right.

In, out, in, out, in, out.

What the hell am I doing sitting here in my office counting my—?

Whoops, I'm not thinking about breathing. I'm thinking about this exercise.

Okay, back to breathing.

In, out, in, out—

Who's that? Ah, Katy. I wonder if she's finished those letters?...

Stop. Back to breathing, Yeah, 1 in, 1 out, 2 in, 2 out—

My foot's going to sleep. Okay, shift position.

Back to breathing, 1 in, 1 out, 2 in, 2 out, 3 in, 3 out, 4 in, 4 out.

Hey! I made it to four! But thinking about making it to 4 isn't focusing on breathing, is it?

Okay, back. 1 in, 1 out, 2 in, 2...

No ordinary human can maintain a pure focus for more than about 12 seconds. The point of this exercise in this form is to learn that fact, to accept that limit, and to practice returning your focus quickly and without fuss. Pretty soon you'll be spending an appreciable amount of time actually focused on your breathing. At the same time, you'll acknowledge distractions more and more quickly. Finally, it's almost instantaneous. You're not locked in a single-minded trance, you're comfortably aware of everything that's going on around you, and you're productively focused on what you are doing.

The conceptual lens of artful making here generates suggestions quite different from those emerging from management research. Recent studies indicate that time pressure and during-work interruptions have a negative impact on an employee's creative cognitive activities;[8] some researchers therefore suggest *protecting* creative workers from time pressures and interruptions. But the theater's success in producing high-quality creative products under severe deadlines, and its method (rehearsal), which is characterized by constant interruption, are at odds with these findings and recommendations.

On reflection, we can see why. Confronted with fixed deadlines, time pressures, and continuous distractions, theater professionals have adapted by learning to control focus. As we shall see in the next chapter, rehearsal in fact thrives on various kinds of interruption, such as the director's constant tinkering with the positions of actors in the *Streetcar* example of Chapter 1. Interruption—better thought of as the introduction of new material—gives the actor more to think about, more interesting problems to solve. In doing so, it fuels innovation. Rather than trying to avoid these and other interruptions, actors acquire the ability to shift their focus rapidly to important matters. There's no reason business people and organizations can't do the same.

Confronted with fixed deadlines, time pressures, and continuous distractions, theatre professionals have adapted by learning to control focus. Rather than trying to avoid interruptions, actors acquire the ability to shift their focus rapidly to important matters.

"Keep your eye on the ball" is a mantra for any game where you hit or catch a ball. In the batter's box, Pete Rose used to whip his head around, watching the baseball clear into the catcher's mitt. That's focus: clearing the mind of distractions by filling it with a chosen object of attention. Learning to focus begins with simple exercises, like counting your breaths—as free as possible of any distracting content—and progresses to become an impressive and useful capability.

SIR ALEC GUINNESS AND THE CHALLENGE OF CONTROL BY RELEASE

When control by restraint comes from within, as when a baseball pitcher loses focus and ends up in a mess, it's usually because an inadvertent focus (that runner in scoring position) creates tension or inhibition rather than release. Theatre lore is full of stories about a version of this problem called "The Second Night Letdown." The audience loves you on opening night. The next night, you eagerly anticipate the great response, and nothing happens. Silence. You can't catch a cold. The great British actor Sir Alec Guinness (Obiwan Kenobi in *Star Wars*) tells a story of a time early in his career when he was cast in a play with Edith Evans.

He was especially anxious to please this great lady; she had befriended him. He got a nice laugh on his exit opening night. He looked for a sign of approbation from Dame Edith, but she didn't seem to have noticed. On the next night, he confidently expected his laugh, but it wasn't there. The audience sat, unmoved. He was mortified, but not downcast, determined to get back the laugh. A week went by, then two. Finally Dame Edith stopped him as he came offstage. "You've lost your laugh," she said, "and you've no idea why." He agreed, utterly dejected, having second thoughts about a career in show business. "It's because you expected it, and you didn't do whatever it was that got the laugh in the first place. Never mind. It will come back. It's there somewhere, in you, and it will come back. And when it does, in about three weeks, I'd say, you'll know what you did, and you'll never lose it again."

Dame Edith was right. The tension of expectation, which he didn't even know he had, degraded his performance. In artful making terms, the actor's anticipation of the laugh had set up a preconception, a restraint that got in his way. On opening night, he acted freely, spontaneously, guided only by the given circumstances and the experiences of rehearsal. The second night, his desire to get the laugh again shifted his focus and inhibited his acting. The sight of him thinking about the previous night's laugh didn't strike the audience as funny. His desire to do it right interfered with doing it right.[9]

THE DIRECTOR'S/MANAGER'S ARTFUL LEVER: FOCUSING THE GROUP

A director/manager cannot necessarily know what workers are doing, cannot tell them what to do, but can often influence their focus. Focus is hard for individuals, as we have seen. It's even harder for organizations. But through influence on focus, good directors/managers can lead the group to release in productive directions, into territory rich with potential.

We've seen that at the individual level, focus is a skill that can be learned and practiced. Actors can be comfortably aware of everything that's going on around them while remaining focused. A manager can help a team learn to focus in a roughly similar way. There's no shortage of examples of organizations with scat-

A principle of honoring limitations, acknowledging distractions, and returning to focus can work in an organizational unit as well as in a theatre ensemble.

tered focus, doing many things all at once and none of them well. Viewed through the artful making lens, this is a problem, not of the damage done by time pressures or interruptions, but of an inability to return wandering attention. A principle of honoring limitations, acknowledging distractions, and returning to focus can work in an organizational unit as well as in a theatre ensemble, as we shall see from an example.

SAVING APOLLO 13: GENE KRANZ AS ENSEMBLE DIRECTOR

Gene Kranz, Mission Director for the ill-fated Apollo 13, led what is certainly one of history's most impressive efforts at innovation under time pressure in response to unexpected events. Most people know the story: On April 13, 1970, 55 hours into the journey to the moon, 200,000 miles from Earth, a wiring defect in one of the spacecraft's liquid oxygen tanks triggered an explosion. Moments later, Jim Lovell, in command of Apollo 13, uttered his calm and now famous words: "Okay Houston, we've had a problem here."

In the next few difficult moments, controllers watched as the craft's oxygen level declined. The ship's fuel cells depended on this disappearing oxygen. The team worked through several faulty hypotheses about what might be wrong, forming then discarding them quickly. No one could see a pattern. They received telemetry readings that should have been impossible. Kranz reports in his autobiography that the group nevertheless displayed "spectacular" teamwork as they coordinated efforts, managing the flow of data, solving problems, fighting what Kranz called "a delaying action."[10] After about 15 minutes, Lovell reported that he could see gas venting into space. The moon landing instantly became a "no-go." All efforts focused now on getting the crew safely back to Earth. Given the damage they could infer from their readings and Lovell's observation, they knew that wouldn't be easy.

The team worked together through numerous difficult choices, operating "outside of all known design and test boundaries of the space systems."[11] They decided to return Apollo 13 to earth via a trajectory around the moon, instead of turning immediately back. They used the moon landing craft as a lifeboat for the astronauts when the primary spacecraft lost its oxygen supply. They forged an ad hoc adapter to solve a problem with the moon landing craft's breathing apparatus (we'll have more to say about this story later). As the damaged, jury-rigged spacecraft neared home, the team figured out how to use a heater cable rigged backwards to charge the main spacecraft batteries from the moon landing craft batteries, something "never envisioned." On the final approach, they corrected a shallow re-entry angle, saving the ship from skipping into space. On April 17, 1970, almost 90 hours after the explosion, the astronauts re-entered Earth's atmosphere. The usual radio blackout ensued, scheduled to last about three minutes. At the four-and-a-half-minute point, just as everyone began to fear the worst, a recovery plane spotted the spacecraft's parachutes. Apollo 13 was home.

In the hours that followed the explosion on Apollo 13, Gene Kranz directed the focus of his highly talented group with great expertise. At times he used abrupt commands such as, "Close it," or, "It'll take too much."[12] He relied on the talents and skills of his team members, guaranteed them that their decisions would not be second-guessed, and acknowledged the legitimacy of exploring options that might not work. But when necessary he turned the focus of the group.

THE DIRECTOR'S/MANAGER'S SOURCE OF AUTHORITY

The tricky thing for an artful manager is that the group's focus is partly a product of its own iterative process. The director/manager must encourage and support the group's trust in the process, must earn the workers' respect, and must help the group regain focus when they wander, as they naturally will. Group members must accept the manager's authority to direct focus or the artful making process comes apart. If the manager's attempts to influence the group's focus seem like random edicts, we are suddenly back in compliance

Group members must accept the manager's authority to direct focus or the artful making process comes apart.

mechanism territory. Kranz could brusquely redirect the focus of his group because he had earned the team's respect.

In many smoothly operating creative groups, focus *is* controlled, but not by any particular member of the group, not even the director/manager. The group may at times assign rights to control focus to a leader like Kranz. But if they don't and the manager tries to take control, you either get a revolt, like the one at Sun, or malicious compliance, which usually involves what is sometimes called "soldiering," or "gaming."[13] In a healthy ensemble, focus is organic, maintained in the making process itself, which, being iterative, provides practice as well. Focus can be influenced, but not ordered about.

The iterative structure of artful making itself assists the director/manager in maintaining an artful form of control. Rehearsal consists of an ongoing sequence of runs of a scene during which all assume that the director will take a leadership role in making suggestions and mediating conflicts. In software development, the periodic (sometimes daily) builds of a prototype product provide similar opportunities for management guidance. As we shall see in the next chapter, workers' assumptions (about how different visions of the emerging product will gather together into new versions) are also part of the rigorous discipline within artful making; *reconceiving*, the artful way of working, combines with Release and direction of focus to achieve precision.

THE PRECISION OF CONTROL
BY RELEASE

Precision in Release arises from the iterative process of doing and doing again, each iteration different, exploring until the surrounding space is very familiar; perfecting your "mechanics" while freeing yourself from "mechanisms." The flawless execution of an actor hitting the mark, releasing into a dramatic moment, precisely on cue, time after time, includes within it the history of all the experiences leading up to that particular moment, all the apparent failures that have been built on and included as material. Lee once watched a designer at work whose uncanny prowess made clear the connection between past exploration (practice) and Release:

> The designer stood in the middle of a huge piece of muslin, the backdrop curtain for an opera. He had a small drawing in his hand, a cartoon, with a grid of squares lightly penciled over it. The cartoon represented the city skyline he was to paint on this enormous area. He had a piece of chalk jammed in the end of a four-foot-long bamboo stick; he could draw on the floor without bending over. Looking at the cartoon, he positioned himself in the middle of the drop, put the chalk on the floor, and took three quick steps backward. I didn't see any part of him move, except for the steps backward, but there on the cloth was a curvy chalk line. He went back to his place, and did it again. Another curvy chalk line, this one completing the outline of a symmetrical tower, an onion-shaped minaret. To my eye the tower looked perfect, its halves exactly similar, balanced. How long did it take him to be able to do that?

The designer's movements were simple, free of tension. But the control that allowed this simplicity and freedom of movement was sophisticated and hard-won, a consequence of many iterations—individual rigor drawn from iterative experience yielding great precision. The descriptive motto here is attributed to Martha Graham, the famous choreographer: "Technique is the dancer's freedom." Lee saw the designer take three amazing steps. For the designer, it might have been the 8,394th iteration, no two of them exactly alike, each of them part of the reason he could do this one so simply. Taken together, they provided the basis for his precise skill.

CONTROL BY RELEASE

As we noted in the introduction to this book, our research project began with a telephone conversation about controlling knowledge workers. Rob asked Lee about an interesting way he had of talking about control in the theatre. In the event Rob remembered, Lee borrowed a pen from a student, gripped it tightly in his hand, and waved that hand in the air. "See this pen?" he said. "I'm controlling it." He swooped it around like a fighter plane. "It's doing exactly what I want it to do." Then he held the pen out in front of him. "Now look; I'm going to control it some more." And he dropped the pen. It fell to the floor and bounced. He picked it up and repeated the gesture. The pen bounced again, quite differently. "See that? It did what I wanted it to, each time."[14]

This is the essence of control by release. Control by turning loose within well-understood given circumstances, reducing artificial tension, ridding yourself of the need to comply with externally imposed mechanisms and criteria. Control by trusting the process. This doesn't mean that anything goes. Kranz, working within the process, brusquely shut down certain behaviors in his meetings, just as a director, like Abigail Adams, will sometimes say "No" to a particular choice or direction. When it's working, the process governs artful behavior better than the best compliance mechanism.

Artful control ensures the quality of Release, which is fundamentally essential to artful making. The spontaneity of each worker's wholly honest and unrehearsed response to the others (the pen bounces differently every time) provides

> This is the essence of control by release. Control by turning loose within well-understood parameters. Control by trusting the process. This doesn't mean anything goes.

room for the creation of methods and ideas no one knew they had, but which are all contained within the given circumstances of the task at hand. The pen always falls; it always bounces.

The director of *Streetcar* didn't interfere with Stanley and Mitch horsing around. She knew that the norms the group had established—that it was her job to maintain and protect—would guide them, and that they would find their way. These norms are like the gravity in Lee's story of dropping the pen. They govern outcomes in a way that the director/manager intends, but can't exactly predict. In business, there are concrete steps we can take to create a context to take the place of gravity: Empower team members to explore; set up low-stakes situations in which everyone can create outrageous thoughts without fear; be available and approachable; earn influence within the group; help the group rehearse a full range of activities and responses the organization might be called on to make; and, make a point of helping them acknowledge inevitable distractions and return to focus on the important issues.

Actors and directors, team members and supervisors, engaged in artful work, need work conditions and methods that liberate rather than stifle creativity. They need to drop the pen, not clutch it. They must have confidence in their freedom and will do their best work in conditions that some people might find disorderly. Artists as a class (not unlike other creative knowledge workers) are notoriously unresponsive to coercion. Each has individual methods and disciplines. Theatre practice accepts these difficulties and reconceives them as opportunities, not problems. Enlightened theatres might choose the members of an ensemble so as to emphasize these difficult characteristics, not reduce them.[15]

In the next chapter, we will take up the following questions: How can apparently incompatible group members combine in collaborative efforts to produce a dynamic, yet rigorously disciplined, process? How can we emulate the discipline of gravity and its liberating power?

ENDNOTES

1. Robert D. Austin and Patrick D. Larkey, "Performance Based Incentives in Knowledge Work: Are Agency Model's Relevant?" *International Journal of Business Performance Management*, 2, no. 1/2/3 (2000) p. 57.

2. Michael A. Hiltzik, *Dealers of Lightning: Xerox PARC and the Dawn of the Computer Age* (New York: HarperCollins, 1999) pp. 145–146.

3. *http://news.bbc.co.uk/2/hi/world/americas/1263917.stm* provides an account of a modern, high-tech company boss who takes such an approach.

4. Austin and Larkey (2000).

5. Tom DeMarco, as quoted in Robert D. Austin, *Measuring and Managing Performance in Organizations* (New York: Dorset House, 1996) p. 113.

6. Robert D. Austin, "The People's Light and Theatre Company" (Harvard Business School case no. 600-055, 2000). Bradley's choice of Toyota as his auto-making example is unfortunate as Toyota's process is arguably the most artful of all automakers. Nevertheless, his point is clear.

7. Richard Sandomir, "Lots of Waggles to See, but Little Suspense," *New York Times* (June 17, 2002) p. D4.

8. Teresa M. Amabile et al., "Time Pressure and Creativity in Organizations: A Longitudinal Field Study" (Harvard Business School working paper 02-073, 2002).

9. Alec Guinness, *Blessings in Disguise* (New York: Alfred A. Knopf, 1986) p. 158.

10. Gene Kranz, *Failure is Not an Option: Mission Control from Mercury to Apollo 13 and Beyond* (New York: Simon and Schuster, 2000) p. 313.

11. Kranz, p. 318.

12. Kranz, p. 321.

13. Robert Kanigel, *The One Best Way: Frederick Taylor and the Enigma of Efficiency* (New York: Viking, 1997) p. 203.

14. I'm indebted to Milton Katselas, a remarkable acting teacher, for this demonstration of control by release (LD).

15. The idea of combining people who aren't likely to see eye-to-eye to yield better creative outcomes has been suggested by many researchers in this area. For example, Dorothy Leonard and Walter Swap have pointed out the advantages of "creative abrasion" in groups in their book *When Sparks Fly: Igniting Creativity in Groups* (Boston: Harvard Business School Press, 1999).

7 ARTFUL MAKING RECONCEIVES; INDUSTRIAL MAKING REPLICATES

B oth artful and industrial making use repeated actions. In artful making, we've been calling them "iterations" but of course industrial making also repeats again and again. There's an important difference, though, in the nature of the repeated actions. Industrial making strives for consistency with a pre-conceived plan or specification. Artful making, in contrast, strives for transformation, for freedom from conformance with preconceptions, toward creating anew. We call industrial repetition *replicating*. Artful making repetition requires that its makers incorporate into their own work the work of others. We call this *reconceiving*.[1]

Simply put, reconceiving takes conflicting circumstances, materials, and potential outcomes, and makes from them a new set of circumstances, materials, and outcomes. These new circumstances, materials, and outcomes tend to be more valu-able than the preceding ones, but not every time. Some itera-tions "regress" to a lower value, producing prototypes that don't work as well as earlier ones. Progress tends to be incremental; but now and then reconceiving yields innovative leaps that surprise everyone. We can explore the fuller meaning of

> Industrial making strives for consistency with a preconceived plan or specification—*replicating*. Artful making, in contrast, strives toward transformation, toward freedom from conformance with preconceptions, toward creating anew—*reconceiving*.

reconceiving, and its relevance to business, by examining how actors might rehearse a scene from *Hamlet*, reconceiving its performance into a new and unique version during each run.

RECONCEIVING HAMLET

When an actor begins rehearsing the role of Hamlet, he sets out to create a Hamlet different from (and better than) any that has gone before. While the script provides materials and a basic form, it can become any number of plays, depending on a host of factors, especially the actors involved. These plays and the characters in them will be very different from one another. For example, Richard Burbage, the tall, slightly fat leading actor in the company Shakespeare wrote for, made the first Hamlet. The script has several teasing references to him being out of condition, not ready for a vigorous sword fight. Nearly 400 years later, in the 20th Century, Lawrence Olivier and Richard Burton were both short men, stocky but by no means slightly fat. Olivier's Hamlet appeared delicate, slender, and gorgeously handsome. Burton's was tough, blocky, and athletic, spoiling for a fight. At one point, Burton jumped up on a table in a single bound. Olivier, no less athletic a man, would not do that. Nor would John Gielgud, who practically sang the role. Nichol Williamson growled it in a guttural North Country dialect. In short, there are as many possible Hamlets as there are actors to make them. It follows that there are as many plays called *Hamlet* as there are theatres to make them and audiences to experience them.

Although we've said this before, it bears repeating here: Whether in business or the arts, an artful making process can take many possible successful directions. It isn't a matter of searching for the only right way to do something. There are always many things that can be made.

Rehearsals are full of unknowns. Consider, for example, the unpredictable chemistry among the players as they work. Sometimes the actors know each other, may even have worked together before. But often they are strangers. There's an edgy quality to the atmosphere, full of ambiguity, uncertainty, a sense that anything can happen. The actors have different methods of working, but all methods derive from a requirement that they become familiar with the others and continually *reconceive* what they're doing *to include others' work as part of their own.*

Here's how that might happen between two actors: George plays Hamlet, the prince, in love with Ophelia. Emily plays Ophelia, the chamberlain's daughter, in love with Hamlet. The actors have never met. They have each read the script

> George doesn't get to put up his hand and say, "I'm sorry, but that's not how I see Ophelia; please change according to my ideas." Instead, George's professional duty is clear: "I have no idea what Emily's going to do; I better be on my toes here."

at home and prepared for rehearsal, independently. At the first rehearsal, the entire cast sits around the table and reads the script aloud.

In George's solo preparation of Hamlet, he assumed a quiet, shy Ophelia, and he's formed some preliminary attitudes toward her based on that assumption. When they meet at the table, the first thing George notices is that Emily isn't shy at all. In fact, she's brash, even pushy. George wonders idly how Emily will put herself under wraps to play the delicate Ophelia. He's soon astonished to discover that she won't be doing anything like that, that she intends to play Ophelia in a bold, in-your-face manner. George is even more astonished to hear the director support Emily in her choices.

As an ensemble member, George doesn't get to put up his hand and say, "I'm sorry, but that's not how I see Ophelia; please change according to my ideas."[2] Instead, George's professional duty is clear: "I have no idea what Emily's going to do; I better be on my toes here." Every time they get together, Emily will surprise George, and George will have to scramble to accommodate her, just as a boyfriend would if the given circumstances were real.

In the meantime, of course, Emily came to rehearsal with the idea that Hamlet would be a tweedy, insecure academic type, and she's equally astonished by George's brusque, dashing man of action. It's entirely possible that the director will have still different ideas about both characters.

Managers will recognize this kind of reconceiving. It's exactly what competitive markets require of them on a regular basis. Examples of the need to reconceive are everywhere in business. When Charles Schwab Corporation decided in 1997 to offer a low, fixed price for Internet-based stock trades, accompanied by a full complement of the firm's customer service options, the unexpected move demanded reaction by other firms.[3] Merrill Lynch, a longtime opponent of Internet stock trading, eventually matched Schwab's price and took actions of its own that caused Schwab to scramble in response.

The dynamic of competitive markets that forces constant reconceiving, move and countermove, has been much celebrated in business and economic history. Joseph Schumpeter called it "creative destruction," and described it as a process that "incessantly revolutionizes the economic structure *from within*, incessantly destroying the old one, incessantly creating a new one."[4] When managers attempt the difficult process of adjusting assumptions and expectations, of remaking their companies and themselves, they are not unlike George and Emily at work on *Hamlet*. Most business readers will be able to think of examples in their own experience, either inside or outside their companies, in which coming to resolution on some issue was primarily a matter of evolving a coherent form out of disparate expectations. Some may also remember less than successful ways such a process worked in a business setting.

In business and theatre, sometimes the reconceiving required involves this sort of response to each other's differing actions and assumptions. But the applicability of reconceiving in business is much more general. Reconceiving may also be aimed at incorporating, not just the actions of others in the immediate process, but also a completely unexpected event or outcome coming at you from the outside. During our field studies, while watching a People's Light public performance of *The Road to Mecca* by Athol Fugard, a play we observed in rehearsal, Rob witnessed a remarkable example of reconceiving in response to an unexpected event:

I sat in just the right spot to see all of this. One of the characters was setting a table—plates, cutlery, and glasses with stems—while conversing with another character. At a tense moment in the conversation, the actor setting the table accidentally bumped a glass with the back of her hand, causing it to tumble onto the seat of a chair, on its way to the floor. Now obviously this could have been very disruptive. Broken glass all over the stage; what do you do with that? But she incorporated it into the performance. The chair had a cushion, so the glass bounced. She caught the glass mid-bounce and then froze her gaze on the other character, as if the whole thing were a reaction to what had just been said. No way had she rehearsed knocking the glass off the table and catching it on the bounce; but when it happened, she made it a part of her work.

The actor dealt with the glass falling off the table in a way that made the accident part of the play. When confronted with the unexpected in any form, whether the choice of another person or events in the environment, the artful making reflex accepts, incorporates, and transforms the altered circumstances into new possibilities. Of course, no actor could knock the glass off the table and catch it every time, but her glare lasted the rest of the run. As we'll see in Chapter 9, this openness to the unexpected embodies an attitude toward uncertainty quite different from an industrial one.

RECONCEIVING TO RECOVER APOLLO 13

When an in-flight explosion crippled Apollo 13, one of the desperate problems was the failure of the scrubbers, machines that remove carbon dioxide from the cabin air, making it safe to breathe again.[6] The filters in the landing craft scrubbers were never intended to support all three astronauts for the entire mission; when they had to move to the landing craft, to use it as a lifeboat, they used up the filters too quickly. They had no spares. The command spacecraft scrubbers had filters, but different contractors built the command and landing crafts, so the filters were incompatible.

Gene Kranz, the Mission Director, assembled a team of engineers down on Earth. They gathered around a pair of scrubbers and filters, like the ones in the ship, and what looked like a pile of random junk. The scrubbers were spares of the ones on the ship, typical NASA engineering: lightweight mechanical perfection. The pile was a complete replica of the Apollo 13 cabin inventory, everything from screwdrivers to used sweat socks. The engineers had mere hours in which to design and build an adapter that would allow the landing craft scrubbers to use the command craft filters. Then they had to teach the astronauts how to do the same. If they couldn't, the astronauts would die. Every item in the pile, socks and all, had to be looked at as a possible adapter component; each component of the craft's scrubber had to be looked at to see what qualities it shared with every item in the pile, socks and all. Nothing could be overlooked; any combination of stuff, no matter how unlikely, how bizarre, had to be conceived as a possible adapter.

They did it. "Odyssey, we have scrubber." Out of the detritus, random stuff, and spare equipment aboard the spacecraft, the engineers fashioned a gizmo that scrubbed carbon dioxide out of the air. They created something entirely new, an adapter never before seen, an assembly of junk. They had thoroughly, creatively, reconceived the function of each item they used. The assembly as a whole contained arrangements, combinations of ingredients, never before imagined by anyone.

Our admiration and wonder at the high stakes (life or death of astronaut heroes) and the flashiness of the task (making a complex machine out of cabin trash) can obscure the main point of this story: In creating something entirely new under great time pressure and on cue—this team had to be creative, or else—the artful accomplishment of Kranz and his team of engineers was not the scrubber adapter, but *the team that could make that scrubber adapter*. Theatre artists call such a team an ensemble, and the ways of working that make an ensemble combine into one of the main qualities of artful making.

The difficulty of making an ensemble is a level of magnitude greater than making a scrubber adapter. The adapter, after all, uses physical materials that, within their limits, do exactly what they are told and don't have needs, fears, and skills. They get along with each other, again within their limits. Above all, they don't each have ideas about how to do the work or about the kind of scrubber adapter they want to be. People are the main material for an ensemble. They must be led, not slammed together; managed, not manipulated.

People are the main material for an ensemble. They must be led, not slammed together; managed, not manipulated.

The Differences Between Reconceiving and Replicating

We contrast reconceiving with *replicating*, the fundamental act of industrial making. Replication creates circumstances, materials, and outcomes that conform as exactly as possible to an objective or specification defined in advance. An automobile assembly line, for instance, might replicate Ford Taurus LXs with standard options in spruce green clearcoat metallic. The makers intend to make all such vehicles identical, even though they may be only every fifth car on the line for two days each month. Or, consider the Interactive Voice Response (IVR) system that you hear when you call your bank: It replicates the service of providing balance information. The makers intend to serve every balance inquiry in exactly the same way (except for actual dollar amounts retrieved at the end). If the outcomes of replication are not identical when we intend them to be, we say we have a "quality problem." Much of the conceptual machinery of industrial making focuses on perfecting replication, to enhance efficiency and avoid quality problems.[6]

Replicating and reconceiving differ in what they use as a primary "referent" while they move toward valuable outcomes. The primary referent used in replicating is the specification, the blueprint, the planned description of what the outcome *should* be. Replication strives toward a specification by following a procedure defined in advance. The primary referent used in reconceiving is "what we did last time." In agile software development, for example, the previous version of the computer code is the primary referent for the next version. In the scene from Hamlet, the way the actors just did it is the primary referent for the way they will do it next.

THE CAPABILITIES OF RECONCEIVING AND REPLICATING

Processes that reconceive have different capabilities than those that replicate. For example:

- *Reconceiving handles unanticipated demands; replicating does not*—If you call your bank with an unusual request, that IVR system probably can't address it. You'll have to get a person on the line (if that's possible!). If the bank's people systems include a capacity to reconceive the bank's responses to include your needs, you may get satisfaction. The person on the line might be empowered to innovate, to reconceive the situation and create a response never offered before. The new response might be quite similar to past responses, or it might be very different. But it can happen without being anticipated.[7]

- *Reconceiving can produce an infinite set of outcomes; replicating can produce only the set of outcomes planned in advance*—A car emerging from a replicating assembly plant will appear in one of several pre-set colors—say, red, green, beige, blue, or silver. If it doesn't, there's a quality problem. There's no ability within a replicating process to produce an in-between outcome, an unplanned variation (like a car that's a little darker green). Reconceiving, on the other hand, routinely and appropriately produces unplanned variations, outcomes of slightly different character every time.

- *Reconceiving means never having to say you're "finished"*—The result of reconceiving can never be called "final." The very idea of a "final product" is problematic in artful making. Because there's no *should be*, no static specification, the final product never arrives. We see this in strategy making at companies like Sun as they adjust to rapidly changing business environments. We see it at software companies where the build of a released product is followed by another build of a new product on the way to the next release.

The outcomes of reconceiving may become more and more similar to each other, but they never become identical. "Performance is different than making sure that a Toyota looks the same each time it gets made."[8] The need for differences from iteration to iteration is the reason for reconceiving. Eliminating those differences is never a goal of artful making. Table 7–1 summarizes the distinctions between reconceiving and replicating.

TABLE 7–1 Reconceiving versus Replicating

RECONCEIVING	REPLICATING
Produces outcomes that were not pre-specified	Produces pre-specified outcomes
Design and manufacturing are part of each other; the process that produces a desired outcome is the same process by which the desired outcome is discovered	Design and manufacturing are separate, sequential phases; the process for producing the pre-specified desired outcome is also designed in advance
Can produce an infinite number of unique outcomes, including "in-between" outcomes (e.g., a car that is a little darker green than that)	Produces a finite and discrete number of outcomes (e.g., a car in red, green, or blue)
Making processes seek out and are driven by variation	Making processes are buffered against variation
Ongoing adjustment of outcome; notion of a "final product" problematic	Well-defined notion of final product

ARTFUL MAKING AND THE CUSTOMER

This aspect of artful making, that its products are never finished, complicates our usual way of thinking about relationships with customers. In industrial settings, we usually fulfill our obligation by delivering, for an agreed-upon price, a final product that is useful in a way the customer expects. But what does it mean to never be done with the product, never to complete a project so that the customer can "sign off on it?" In Chapter 10, we'll fully address questions of how you budget and pay for artful making, given that it has this "never done" characteristic; for now we note that artful making forces us to reconceive what we mean by "product." Fortunately, the reconceived notion we're proposing is not alien to business and is even becoming somewhat commonplace: that the real product is not a thing, but an experience, an interaction between a thing and a customer.[9] Once again, the theatre example is a good fit for how we need to think about this in a business context.

Each audience for a play production is different from any other. Friday/Saturday night audiences tend to be tired, overfed, even a little drunk. The streams of energies moving back and forth between these audiences and the actors are quite different from those on, say, Sunday night, when the spectators tend to be fans, very interested, alert, and responsive. The two audiences could hardly be more different, but they resemble each other more than they resemble the high school kids who come at 10 a.m. on some days. We conceive the play, the theatre's product-for-sale, as made out of both production and audience. Hence, different audiences result in different plays.

W. Edwards Deming introduced the concept of a manufacturing process that ends with a satisfied customer and applied it to the sequence of internal systems at a factory: supplier, maker, customer. Agile software developers modify this sequence, adding the concept of an active customer, one with evolving needs. And, play making takes these ideas to their natural conclusion, conceiving the audience (customer) as material out of which a play is made.

For artful makers, customers are integral to successful making—"co-producers," to use an expression that has acquired recent popularity in business research literature. The artful maker never stops reconceiving the product because he or she includes an ever-changing customer as material and as part of the process. The product itself isn't a single thing you can point to or count. It's the totality of the interaction among the made thing and whoever experiences it. This interaction might include industrial replication of an object for sale. Automakers use industrial methods when they make cars, but they increasingly conceive of their product—appropriately, we believe—as the customer's experience of owning a car. This experience might even span a series of cars, each industrially made by the company.

NEVER-DONE, CONSTANTLY IMPROVING DEVELOPMENT

Trilogy CEO Joe Liemandt, talking about the company's approach to software development, explains why the products of artful making are never finished:

> We believe the number-one issue for software development is you don't know the spec *or* the spec changes. You thought you knew it, but by the time you deliver it, it's going to change. So you get to the question, "What's the bigger problem, making sure you are building it right? Or that you are building the right thing?". . .What we do, Fast Cycle Time, it's about building the right thing, because that's where most things go wrong. . . And because of our process orientation, where we look at the whole end-to-end process over a ten-year period, we say *we never want to be done.* I never want a system to stop being built. We want to continue to rev it every three to six months, forever. The key to that is: "Are you trying to automate a business process that's highly valuable? One that you always want to continue to improve to stay aligned with the business?" [If so,] you want to continue to build the technology under it. Which keeps providing more and more business value. That really is our methodology. We never want to be done providing new business value.[10]

RECONCEIVING VERSUS COMPROMISING

In daily life and politics, we use compromise as one of our main categories for thinking about agreements or conflicts. We know compromise as a primary tool of management and the principle activity of representative government. In a simple conflict between two people or groups, the efficacy of this method, the necessity of it, seems clear. You say five, they say three; let's compromise on four. In a compromise, each party gives up something while retaining an acceptable core of the position. In some contexts, compromise is an excellent method of working out conflicting actions and mutually exclusive requirements.

Compromise also has negative connotations. When we're talking about principles, about what we know to be true, we abhor compromise. If you deplore capital punishment or defend the right to bear arms, you may not agree to compromise your position. Moreover, just about anyone knows examples of administrative procedures, policies, rules, and even products that have been compromised along too many directions to remain effective. We often see such ineffective outcomes used as an argument for strong, control-by-restraint leadership.

Compromising, in the usual sense of the word, doesn't make sense in artful making, either. It may seem on first glance that George and Emily compromised in their work on *Hamlet*. That's not what they did. When George crosses to sit on the bench while Emily wishes he would remain standing center stage, the compromise (having him sit in the thin air midway between the bench and center stage) isn't an option. Instead, she adapts to his move, making a gesture he's never seen before and to which he must in turn adapt, and so on and so on. They don't compromise their ideas; they make new ones. They both reconceive what they're doing, creating a brand-new interaction with its own coherent relationship to everything else. This is a much stricter requirement than "splitting the difference." The new made thing that results from collaborative reconceiving never settles down. The form of what's being made will, given the interdependency of all its parts, continue growing to accommodate whatever happens during the making. It will be far less predictable (and far more interesting) than a product of compromise.

In artful making, the very act of makers accommodating each other changes the nature of the work itself; this change in turn requires change in the individual goals and methods of every ensemble member. The resulting process requires each person to constantly change his or her mind in response to the actions of others. The work goes slowly, with difficulty (and to the impatient observer, inefficiently). Its end cannot be predicted, is more a result than a goal. It's a laborious, often frustrating, but ultimately deeply satisfying movement toward real unity.[11]

This unity of the developing product, process, or solution is also of primary importance in knowledge work. Any manager can cite examples of projects or products so compromised as to be badly suited to their purpose. Sometimes we deride such products by saying they were "designed by committee." Organizations can produce balky, glued-together outcomes when they don't fully appreciate the interdependency of process, materials, form, and purpose required in artful making.

Artful making avoids locking in too early, primarily because it places such great importance on moving toward unity. In many business settings, this approach will seem chaotic and uncertain, even when it's working well. The presumption is that if we don't lock in, if we don't make compromises, if we don't quickly commit to decisions and quit changing our minds, we won't achieve our objective on time. If we don't know the objective in detail, well, that's only more evidence that our methods are unsound. Artful making cannot survive such presumptions. Those who want to make artfully in business must constantly ask themselves whether impatience and yearning for certainty have curtailed important exploration and innovation—whether the impulse to compromise has undermined the fundamental coherence of the product.

ARTFUL COLLABORATION

In artful collaboration, the makers' abilities to release, to control focus, and to reconceive—these work in concert. The heart of collaboration is release without inhibition into unpredictable choices. Those choices generate challenges for other collaborators, materials that they must include in their own work. In an artful process, independent artful workers continually interrupt each others' work with new materials that demand reconceiving. Artful makers learn to return to focus. The exercise of this skill results in a kind of concentration that can accommodate new input without interrupting the main flow. Emily doesn't stop her work to remonstrate when George doesn't move as she expected. She carries on, and unless you've seen the previous run-through, you won't notice her busy accommodation to something new. What could be chaotic and disruptive is in fact high-octane fuel for innovation.

> Artful makers must constantly ask themselves whether impatience and yearning for certainty have curtailed important exploration and innovation—whether the impulse to compromise has undermined the fundamental coherence of the product.

Nothing here should be construed to mean that interruptions are always useful in a rehearsal or meeting. Also, it's important to remember that workers support their work with intensive homework, often done alone. In play making, this means learning lines and creating a backstory (recall from our *Streetcar* example in Chapter 1 the efforts of the actors playing Mitch and Stanley to make up a story that explained their friendship despite the disparity in their ages). In idea making, it means developing a thorough command of the relevant information needed to address the meeting's issues.

Workers faced with reconceiving must have absolute freedom to respond to the work of others. Everyone must honor the impulsive, the unusual. In the next chapter, we will turn to a discussion of the conditions in which we can achieve such freedom and do artful work.

ENDNOTES

1. Some of the early work on reconceiving as applied to business was done in collaboration with Jonathan West of HBS. In the fall of 1999, West and the two authors of this book presented "Production as Serial Reconception" to the innovation seminar at HBS. A working paper, "Beyond Manufacturing," was also a product of this work.

2. In the commercial theatre, if George was a star or had money in the production, he *could* do this. William Gibson tells this story, starring Henry Fonda, in *The Seesaw Log* (New York: Alfred A. Knopf, 1959).

3. Nicole Tempest and F. Warren McFarlan, "Charles Schwab Corporation (A)" (Harvard Business School case no. 300-024, 1999); Nicole Tempest and F. Warren McFarlan, "Charles Schwab Corporation (B)" (Harvard Business School case no. 300-025, 1999).

4. Joseph A. Schumpeter, *Capitalism, Socialism, and Democracy* (New York: Harper, 1975; originally published 1942) p. 83.

5. We draw on several sources for this account, including: Gene Kranz, *Failure is Not an Option: Mission Control from Mercury to Apollo 13 and Beyond* (New York: Simon and Schuster, 2000); David M. Upton and Sari Carp, "HMS Thetis and Apollo XIII" (Harvard Business School case no. 696-097, 1996); and *Apollo 13: To The Edge and Back*, a video documentary directed by Noel Buckner and Rob Whittlesey for WGBH Public Television (1994).

6. Replication processes do sometimes, of course, produce multiple, different outcomes (a green car can also be made in blue, for example), but all versions are specified in advance.

7. Employees are not typically given unlimited rights to reconceive. It is unlikely, for example, that bank employee empowerment extends to acts of embezzlement in a bank. In a rehearsal, the script, given circumstances, and other materials act as limiting guides for the actors and director as they reconceive the developing play-to-be.

8. David Bradley, quoted in Robert D. Austin, "The People's Light and Theatre Company" (Harvard Business School case no. 600-055, 2000).

9. B. Joseph Pine, James H. Gilmore, and B. Joseph Pine II, *The Experience Economy* (Boston: Harvard Business School Press, 1999).

10. Liemandt made his comments during a class in July 2001, part of the annual "Delivering Information Services" program at HBS.

11. Mary Follett suggests a similar conception of some political activities in *Dynamic Administration, The Collected Papers of Mary Parker Follett*, eds. Henry C. Metcalf and L. Urwick (London: Sir Isaac Pitman & Sons Ltd., 1941). See especially "Constructive Conflict."

8 ARTFUL MAKING REQUIRES A SECURE WORKSPACE

Artful collaboration requires exposure to risks. There's a risk that superiors, or customers, or others whose opinions matter might disagree with choices we make or opinions we express. Bad things can happen if the project fails to accomplish its "goals." In Chapter 6 we discussed how artful makers release themselves past tensions and inhibitions by using their ability to focus, to direct attention away from the source of inhibitions. Artful managers must also do their part; they must create conditions in which makers can work at risk.

Willingness to work at risk is vital in artful making, in part because exploration is uncomfortable. Exploration requires a willingness to supply partial answers, to float trial balloons, to look goofy, and to get things "wrong." The pre-mission simulations of moon landings for Apollo 11 included several crashes, which led to excruciating days for flight controllers and astronauts. Yet those crashes played a vital role in the ultimate success of the Eagle landing on the moon.[1] And it was important to the effectiveness of the preparation that flight controllers really "feel" these crashes. They experienced the moon landing simulations as actors do the given circumstances of a play, *as if they were real*. Few

> Willingness to work at risk is vital in artful making, in part because exploration is uncomfortable. Exploration requires a willingness to supply partial answers, to float trial balloons, to look goofy, and to get things "wrong."

plays feature characters who have it easy, are really nice, and never suffer. Yet an actor making a character must do the thoughts, feelings, and deeds of that character, *as if they were real*. Even in low-stakes settings, team members need to explore possibilities they'd rather not consider.

Managers can help in this process by making sure exploration doesn't impose unacceptable costs on employees. You can think of this as satisfying the prerequisite conditions for artful making that we discussed in Chapter 4. There we observed that the cost of exploration, part of the cost of iteration, could not be too high or artful making would not work. This chapter addresses the *psychological* cost of exploration. The willingness of employees to work artfully depends partly on whether working conditions sufficiently lower the psychological cost of exploration, and partly on employee willingness to work at risk—on "the edge," as we put it.

SECURING THE WORKSPACE

Creating a secure workspace is one way artful makers make productive the naturally high stakes and inherent risks in their work. W. Edwards Deming said, "No one can put in his best performance unless he feels secure.... Secure means without fear, not afraid to express ideas, not afraid to ask questions."[2] Gene Kranz made certain that everyone could express their opinions freely during the Apollo 13 crisis, even though the stakes in that situation could not have been higher.

As Deming also observed, the forces that disrupt the security of a workspace in business are all too common.[3] An email that recently found its way into the press, originally sent by the CEO of a medical software company to his managers, illustrates the nature of such disruptions. In the email, he threatened to replace managers who could not drive their employees to work hard enough. He promised it would be a very, very long time before he increased company benefits; he said he would judge how his managers were performing in part by whether parking lots at the company were full by 7:30 a.m., and whether they were at least half-full on weekends. He closed his message by reminding managers that they had only two weeks to make effective changes.[4]

With exceptions now and then, a theatre ensemble does its work in a collegial atmosphere of mutual respect and support, as free as possible from fear of failure's ordinary consequences. All the artists work deliberately, methodically to create these conditions. A theatre protects its workspace with a dedicated appreciation for norms and interpersonal boundaries. In a theatre rehearsal, a NASA crisis, or a high-stakes business meeting, interaction must transcend the level of the usual niceties that protect us in most of human affairs. People must voice their opinions freely regardless of consequences, imagined or real. Because we can't afford the everyday social buffers when we are doing the hard, exploratory work of artful making, the sanctity of the workspace and the mutual respect of the ensemble members must substitute for the usual social conventions.

> W. Edwards Deming once wrote, "No one can put in his best performance unless he feels secure.... Secure means without fear, not afraid to express ideas, not afraid to ask questions."

EDMONDSON'S "PSYCHOLOGICAL SAFETY" CONCEPT

Professor Amy Edmondson has studied the importance of a construct she calls "psychological safety," with a particular emphasis on its implications for team learning. This idea, related to the notion of a secure workspace in theatre, is based on the underlying premise that people are naturally inclined to manage others' impressions of them. They avoid actions that might make people think they are ignorant, incompetent, negative, or disruptive. When people try to minimize risk to their image, Edmondson suggests, they undermine the open interaction essential to individual and team learning. To counter this tendency toward risk management, which obstructs learning, organizations sometimes succeed in creating a sense of psychological safety:

> In psychologically safe environments, people believe that if they make a mistake others will not penalize or think less of them for it. They also believe that others will not resent or penalize them for asking for help, information or feedback. This belief fosters the confidence to take the risks described above and thereby to gain from the associated benefits of learning.
>
> I argue that creating conditions of psychological safety is essential for laying an effective foundation for learning in organizations. I further propose that structuring a collective learning process at the team or group level is a second critical element for organizational learning, and that a compelling goal is necessary for motivating this collective learning process.[5]

Although Edmondson's insistence that a goal is necessary may at first seem contrary to our suggestion that artful making is about transcending and continuously transforming detailed objectives, in fact it's not. A goal can be quite abstract, reachable by many paths, and the ones Edmondson identifies are. She writes of healthcare workers' shared goal of doing good for their patients. This is much the same kind of goal as to create an excellent play. Furthermore, an ongoing transformation of instrumental goals is inherent in the collective learning process she describes.

Empirical evidence from studies of teams in hospitals shows that people were more likely to speak up about concerns or errors when they felt safe. More important for our argument, they also proposed more innovations. Psychological safety disappeared when leaders exhibited "autocratic behavior, inaccessibility, or failure to acknowledge vulnerability."[6] Leadership behaviors conducive to psychological safety include demonstrating tolerance for failure, refraining from punitive exercise of power, and participating in team processes rather than imposing rules.

SECURITY BEYOND THE WORKSPACE

We distinguish between a firm's internal workings and its place in the business world. As we write, that business world has suffered serious change and catastrophic losses due to a constellation of events that no one foresaw. Corporations that appeared healthy have vanished; job security in many sectors of the economy seems like a thing of the past, even at senior levels (especially at senior levels, some would say). Artful making has a straightforward role in the history of a firm's relationship to its environment: When conditions meet the prerequisites (see Chapter 4), managers and workers alike can practice artful making in pursuit of a better product. Better products lead to more satisfied customers, higher profitability, and increased value for shareholders. Managers who want to generate higher value for shareholders must figure out a way to make the workspace secure if they want innovation to play a part in value creation (as it probably must).

Corporate and individual accountability are features of artful making, even in theatre. A theatre's management is directly accountable to a board of directors. If things go badly, jobs are at risk. The artists place themselves personally on the line in a way that many business people rarely do, working in the same room with their customers. Fiscal health is a prior condition for artistic freedom. Everyone takes an interest. The "metrics" of artful making are everywhere and unforgiving. And yet, the security of the workspace must be maintained or innovation will shut down.

CREATIVE INTERCHANGE

The creative efforts required to overcome obstacles to artful making can result in what at first seem like miraculous interchanges among ensemble members. Reveling in the safety of the workspace, colleagues who release past their fears and inhibitions enjoy a rapport with one another that many find exhilarating, even addictive. During a rehearsal at People's Light, an observer recorded the following conversation between playwright Lou, director Ken, and actors Tom and

> In a theater rehearsal, a NASA crisis, or a high-performance business team, interaction must transcend the level of the usual niceties that protect us in most of human affairs. Sanctity of workspace and mutual respect of the ensemble members must substitute for the usual social conventions.

Steve; though extremely cryptic, it was in fact a rich exchange of information:

Ken: Try to make this moment...

Tom: Got it.

Ken: Great.

Steve: You know if I...

Ken: Sure, go ahead.

Lou: I like it.

Ken: Let's keep it.

Lou: I'll need to rewrite.

Ken, Tom, Steve: Well... [7]

In these few seconds, Ken begins to suggest something to Tom, a possibility he's noticed in the last run of the scene. He doesn't have to finish his sentence because Tom sees it too. Tom's "Got it" confirms to Ken that, as Ken had suspected, they've both seen the possibility; "Great," Ken responds. Matter resolved. Then Steve starts to offer a suggestion about what he might do given what Ken and Tom just resolved (Steve had followed their brief exchange). Once again, Ken is right with the actor on the next thing to try and says, "Sure, go ahead," keeping that exchange short (they are working within a momentum, keeping the juices flowing). Lou, the playwright, is following the exchange as well. He gives his approval, and Ken, the director, suggests (just confirmation, really, of what they've already all decided) that the choices they've made here, the ideas they're working, should remain in the way they do the scene. Playwright Lou then suggests that he'll write these choices into the script. It's difficult to interpret the "Well..." from Ken, Tom, and Steve, but it's possible that they're not yet sure about writing changes into the script, maybe because things are not through changing.

Kent Beck, a leader of the agile software development movement, reports observable efficiencies like these between "pair programmers" in highly iterative and interactive activities. [8] Interestingly, "extreme programming," the variety of agile software development Beck promotes, includes a philosophy of protecting workers and their workspaces from the kinds of fear-based tactics we described earlier.[9]

WORKING ON YOUR "EDGE"

Securing the workspace isn't all that is needed to get past fear and discomfort to creative performance. The flip side of the coin is the need for individual ensemble members to build up a capacity for working on what we call the *edge*.[10] Learning to work on the edge is a part of learning to achieve reliable innovation, and it's the manager's job to help with this task. The theatre has evolved ways and means to accommodate the natural and healthy anxiety that even artists bring to their creative work.

FINDING A PHYSICAL EDGE

As we found with release, it's best to introduce the idea of an edge in its physical manifestations. From this we can build to a more sophisticated idea of edges that will be of importance in creative business work. Actors learn to work on their edges through exercises like this one:

Bend over at the waist. Flex your knees so that you can put your palms flat on the floor. By straightening your knees, you can now stretch the big muscles at the back of your legs, your hamstrings. There's a point at which this will start to hurt. This minor pain is your edge for this stretch. Now, with your palms still on the floor, focus on and release your hamstrings to allow your legs to straighten a little more, until discomfort urges you to stop. Hold there for a moment. Let go to ease the discomfort. Try it again. Don't force your muscles. Release them.

Most creative work, onstage or in the conference room, takes place at such an edge or just beyond. It's vital at the moment of experiencing an edge that you understand: *This discomfort will never go away.* If you want to become adept at any activity involving change, growth, innovation, or creativity, you'll eventually face up to the fact that edge discomfort is a part of your life. You'll need to be okay with that. You don't want to learn to stretch painlessly. You want to learn to accept the discomfort of an edge as a condition of your work, a sign that you're doing it well. Resistance training is another example. Some weightlifting exercises require working to the point of failure; while the weight or number of repetitions to failure may vary, working to failure is always just that, and it always hurts. Learning your edges doesn't mean that you somehow "conquer" or "overcome" edge discomfort. Conquering, overcoming, and other kinds of clenching are not what we're doing here. A psychological, social, or emotional edge requires the same kind of careful but insistent exercise as a physical edge: learning to be okay with the discomfort of the edge; learning to move the edge outward by releasing into discomfort for controlled periods.

As managers explore edges, for themselves and for their organizations, there are a couple of caveats to keep in mind. First, there's a difference between the discomfort of an edge, and the pain of injury. Whether in an individual or team, edge discomfort is the sign of good work going forward. Whether in muscles or relationships among team members, injury pain, the feeling of damage, is a sign that something's wrong. Physical injury pain usually gives a pretty clear signal. Psychological, social, or emotional injury pain may be less easy to recognize.

Second, and perhaps most important for impatient managers, the edge is not about quantity of work or fear-mongering. You don't reach an edge by threatening your people, by insisting that they work longer hours, or by making sure the parking lot is full on Saturday morning. Artful making is a matter of the risks employees are eager to take, not how much they rush around or how many hours they spend at their desks.

LEARNING TO WORK ON YOUR EDGE

To become expert at working on an edge requires two things. First: practice. The stress of an edge becomes less threatening with practice. Second, much more complex, difficult, and important: self-knowledge. As we have seen, a willingness to work on the edge goes hand-in-hand with a complex notion of safety. Here the notion of a secure workspace and a willingness to work on the edge come together. Ultimately, the security of an artful making workspace arises from self-knowledge, self-trust, and the trust in others that comes from working on an edge together.

> A psychological, social, or emotional edge requires the same kind of careful but insistent exercise as a physical edge: learning to be okay with the discomfort of the edge; learning to move the edge outward by releasing into discomfort for controlled periods.

Actors first encounter this kind of self-knowledge, and consequently improve their ability to work reliably on the edge, through exercises. In the Blind Walk, for example, one person leads a blindfolded person by the hand around a complicated space (the room, the building, the garden). The blindfolded person immediately finds an edge in the amount of trust he or she is willing to accord the leader ("Promise I won't run into anything?"). The leader will find an edge in his/her follower's fear ("How come you don't trust me?"). Actors do this exercise over and over, gradually learning to extend their edge to the point where they can run together at top speed, secure, if edgily apprehensive. Another such exercise, the Trust Circle, in which people allow themselves to fall and be caught by other members of the group, extends the idea of releasing to the edge from the individual to the group.[11]

When leading or catching in the Blind Walk or Trust Circle, you soon resolve to do anything, pay any price, to keep your partner or the faller from harm, to make sure that nothing will interfere with his or her safety (and sense of safety). When you know, deep down *know*, how fully you're resolved to prevent any harm, you begin to understand that your partners can feel the same way, can make the same resolves. As actors practice the Blind Walk, the Trust Circle, and similar exercises, they gradually become good at working on trust edges by understanding themselves. Ensemble members trust each other because each has learned self-trust. The trust deepens as each realizes the extent of the effort that must be made, and makes that effort. The trust becomes mutually reinforcing, interlocking: "If he can do it, so can I"; "If I can do it, so can he"; "If I want her to trust me, I'd better be willing to trust her."

The same kind of understanding extrapolates to the more complex life situations of rehearsal and performance, of meetings and conferences. Business teams can benefit from collective experiences that require individuals to extend themselves, and to rely on others. Exercises are one way to achieve this. But business provides many other opportunities to manage a process in which groups of people are asked to do difficult things together. Management researcher Jeffrey Liker, writing with co-authors, has observed, for example, that Japanese companies and their suppliers intentionally create mutual vulnerabilities in their relationships, opportunities for each to exploit the other. In doing this, they elicit an apparently paradoxical response in which the parties are loathe to exploit their relationship in any way.[12]

LEARNING BY DOING

When we think "about" something, we position ourselves at an intellectual distance from it. This is one of the great skills of being human, and we use it to imagine the future on the basis of the past. It's the heart of planning. We've seen the gradual development in business of a distance between doing (the master machinist) and thinking (the rate clerk with an instruction card). Commercial pressures have led our culture to separate out and privilege thinking about how to do work over the actual doing of it. We've reached a point in this book, though, where we can see ourselves coming full circle, to kinds of work where artful and ancient making meet.

Let's revisit Hugh and his armory. Hugh had no book of instructions, no rate card, for the task of making a harness of armor. He learned his craft by doing, beginning with simple, ancillary tasks. He fed the furnace and pumped its bellows, swept up after the animals; he watched intently while Philip hammered and annealed and hammered some more. He watched that work into his own body until he could hardly stand not doing it himself.

When he got the chance, he expressed what he had learned, not by taking a paper-and-pencil exam, but by heating and pounding a piece of iron.

Many steps in an artful making process will demand Hugh's kind of ancient "thinking" and "learning." The task, the experience, is incommensurate with language, with intellection. It isn't a question of being too complicated to put into words. It's more than that. Something about it is un-word-able. The same thing applies to the processes of focus and release, of finding and exploring your edges. To tell you *about* focus and release, we've suggested an exercise of focus and release. If you read the instructions with a lively and histrionic imagination, you'll know something *about* focus and release, as Hugh knew *about* blacksmithing from watching Philip. The next step is to create ways actually to *do* focus and release.

EGO VERSUS VANITY: GIVING UP SOVEREIGNTY OVER YOUR WORK

Artful making requires building up individual ego in group members, while tearing down vanity. The first step is to learn and internalize the distinction, to reconceive ego and vanity in new terms. Vanity is that inner need to appear before others as we appear to ourselves, or as we'd like to appear to ourselves. Vanity makes you worry about another's opinion of your haircut. Ego, on the other hand, is that sense we have of being a distinct creature in the world, a creature of value. Your ego is who you are, your sense of yourself as an individual, and if it's strong enough, you can live with anyone's opinion of your haircut. If your ego is strong enough, you can belong to a group and recognize that the group is greater than the sum of its parts; that it may not, in fact, have separable parts; and that your success will be measured by the group's success, not by your personal contribution. When you're worried about who did what, you can't make artfully. If your ego is strong enough, you can let go of vanity and release your fear that others won't like what you do. You can do whatever needs to be done.

MAKING AN ENSEMBLE

Let's revisit the *Streetcar* rehearsal we described in Chapter 1. "We have play," said the voice, mimicking the NASA controllers who manage space missions. What exactly did the group "have" that set this rehearsal apart from those preceding it? It certainly wasn't a perfect rehearsal. Actors had stumbled and called for lines; they worked in a bare room without scenery, lights, or sound; they had only bits of costume and substitute props as they moved on a floor plan outlined in colored tape. They weren't done in any sense. There was much left to do—a huge amount really—before opening night.

What they had was Ensemble, the penultimate quality of artful making. The work as a whole, through the collaboration made possible by a willingness to work from release rather than restraint, had become more compelling than the work of any one of the actors. The group had become, in effect, greater than the sum of its parts. The emerging play began to have "a life of its own." When this happens in a group, it can seem amazing and magical to someone outside looking in. But to the actors working at this rehearsal, there was nothing supernatural about it, and no one had organized an extraordinary event (an offsite retreat, for example) to summon it. The artists did their daily work. An observer could recognize the actors' overt behavior: They all moved around the room and talked loudly. To an uninitiated observer, these gestures might add up to an attempted play that got a little better each time they did it, as each actor became more practiced and smoother with lines and movement. The conversations between actors and the director focused on these visible activities: "What if you move down right when you talk to her?"; "How about more anger there? Does that make sense?" Everything seemed to aim at bringing the script to life, at making it into a play.

Beneath the surface, though, lay their constant, tacitly understood target: Ensemble, the quality in the work that the actors (and the observer) could recognize as something special. The actors plied their many invisible skills long, hard, and systematically to achieve it. They would continue to work long, hard, and systematically to maintain it while the play-to-be gradually took shape among them, and later during the run as they reliably made the play with a new audience each night.

We call Ensemble a quality of the work because every moment in an artful making process exhibits it. It cannot be extracted for analysis, because a process without it will no longer be artful making.

> You don't reach the edge by threatening your people, or by making sure the parking lot is full on Saturday morning. Artful making is a matter of the risks people are eager to take, not how many hours they spend at their desks.

This is true of each of the qualities we've mentioned: Release, Collaboration, Ensemble, and Play. None of them can be removed without changing a process from artful making to something else. In addition, the four qualities are interdependent: Anything affecting one affects them all. We'll have more to say about this in Chapter 11.

TWO KINDS OF REALITY

In thinking about what's going on when we create a secure workspace as a part of artful work, it may be useful to think about the similar spaces we create outside of work, in "real" life. Think of family interactions or the delicate rituals of romance. In these settings, many of our gestures are entirely situational, inappropriate in any other context. The gestures of those spaces stay there and don't spill out into the rest of life. We babytalk to the baby, not to the bus driver. This is true also of the workspace for artful making. In a rehearsal this means, for example, that the passion expressed between two actors in a love scene or quarrel is not continued or exploited outside the rehearsal hall. In a brainstorming session, it means your cockamamie idea stays in the room; no one rags on you about it at lunch.

But it doesn't mean that our activities in any of these spaces are insincere, that they're pretending of any kind.

Sometimes we achieve safety in an interaction with others by asserting an artificial status for the interaction. We do this when we say things like, "Let me play devil's advocate here." This announcement distances our true selves from the excitements of a heated discussion among team members; it makes us artificially present rather than really present. But for success at artful making, the interaction has to be real; it can't be any kind of pretending. Rehearsal love or anger must be as "real" as the actors can make it, full and passionate, expressed with support and absolute conviction; the actors must accept each other's real gestures as gifts, as material that will make the scene better. Conducting a discussion over the budget in a similar way will improve the quality of that interaction.

But the reality of a secure workspace isn't the same as the reality of "real life." Actors learn that a passionate love scene in rehearsal or onstage, while real, isn't the same kind of real as the same action would be in real life. Managers and team members also need to understand that heat generated in the workspace as part of an argument on policy is a different order of behavior than similar feelings might be in daily life, even though the two are the same except for the context and purpose. This requires discipline and dedication.

The potential of using two kinds of reality as a way to think about working in the conference room and lab may take some getting used to. The work around the conference table must be as free of pretense as anyone can make it. Artful making work must be as intense and personal as we can make it. And the inevitable creative conflicts that arise between people must be worked out, no matter what. But artful making requires collaboration: reconceiving, not a fight to the death. The brilliant argument mustn't aim at defeating an opponent, but at making a better product. It's an artful maker's gift to his/her partners. At the peak of disagreement, artful makers must be able to embrace that gift and use it to make a new idea of their own. This takes practice that is best done in a situation where the stakes can be lowered as people learn their edges and practice releasing into them.

A Whole Greater than the Sum of its Parts

For most of us, the kind of interaction that happens when working with a really terrific team is work as good as it gets. Talk with a colleague who has been part of a highly effective team and you'll often get a sense that work has never been as gratifying since. This can matter more than money, or

> For most of us, the kind of interaction that happens when working with a really terrific team is work as good as it gets.

promotions, or any of the other conventional trappings of success. People know when they're working well, when they're on fire with excellence. But it doesn't happen in an environment of fear. It doesn't happen unless working on the edge is a possibility.

As the web of associations among people and ideas grows, each member of the ensemble begins to see that the product-to-be they're making every day is in fact something brand new. All begin to feel the power of creativity, of making something that didn't exist before, that couldn't exist without them, that is made of their personal presence, of their *own* work. When the ensemble itself becomes a kind of artwork, when the group members begin to see their particular effort as part of a larger and more expressive whole thing, then that larger thing becomes greater than the sum of the individual contributions. Everyone's desire to share this remarkable, unique creation with others increases the excitement of the approaching "product launch."

As everyone becomes more fully engaged and more deeply attached, each to each other and all to the project, the group becomes an ensemble. The features of this creation elude description: a case of "I can't define it, but I know it when I see it." From outside, spectators can identify in a production that exhibits the quality of Ensemble a sense of unity in purpose and methods, a feeling that what they're observing is indeed unique and precious, and a vivid awareness that what they're observing is being made right this minute. They're present at the creation. This is to say that ensemble work nearly always results in a high-quality product, and a high-quality product nearly always generates the loyal customers that support any successful business enterprise. From within, the production team experiences the quality of Ensemble as a feeling of impending success and a growing sense of happiness at being part of what's unfolding. If the product doesn't find favor in the marketplace, the solidarity of the ensemble and the joy of working help maintain the group's morale and momentum for the next project.[13]

Each person involved in artful making starts out with a preliminary concept of the emerging product. None of these concepts fully survives the process, nor should they. Preconceived ideas, rigid plans and goals, with their inevitable limitations on outcomes, have no place in artful making. In the next chapter, we'll show how artful making incorporates environmental uncertainties within and beyond the workspace into an emerging and unpredictable product.

ENDNOTES

1. Gene Kranz, *Failure Is Not an Option: Mission Control from Mercury to Apollo 13 and Beyond* (New York: Simon and Schuster, 2000) pp. 265–266.

2. W. Edwards Deming, *Out of the Crisis* (Cambridge, Miss.: MIT Press, 1995).

3. Ibid.

4. "Boss's angry e-mail sends shares plunging," Daily Telegraph, London (April 6, 2001), reprinted online at: *http://www.commondreams.org/headlines01/0406-04.htm*. When the e-mail became public, the company's stock lost 22% of its value.

5. Amy C. Edmondson, "Managing the risk of learning: Psychological safety in work teams," *International Handbook of Organizational Teamwork*, ed. M. West; see also Amy C. Edmondson, "Psychological Safety and Learning Behavior in Work Teams," *Administrative Science Quarterly*, 44, no. 4 (1999) pp.

350–383; and Amy C. Edmondson, Richard Bohmer, and Gary P. Pisano, "Disrupted Routines: Team Learning and New Technology Adaptation," *Administrative Science Quarterly,* 46, (2001) pp. 685–716.

6. Ibid.

7. "From People's Light & Theatre Company: 25 Years," People's Light marketing materials.

8. From remarks presented by Kent Beck at the Cutter Summit, April 29–May 1, 2001, Cambridge, MA.

9. Kent Beck, *Extreme Programming Explained: Embrace Change* (Boston: Addison-Wesley, 2000).

10. I'm indebted to Carmelita DiMichael, first a student, then a teacher, for this useful idea (LD). The concept of working on the edge also occurs in the work of Shona L. Brown and Kathleen M. Eisenhardt, and is used in their book, *Competing on the Edge: Strategy as Structured Chaos* (Boston: Harvard Business School Press, 1998). As far as we know, the use of this term in these very different contexts arose completely independently. It's interesting that their intended meanings are nevertheless very similar.

11. The Trust Circle exercise goes like this: Members of a group stand in a circle of no fewer than six, no more than eight. They tighten the circle until everybody's shoulders touch. One person steps into the center of the circle and closes his or her eyes, then two people in the circle reach out and take the hands of the person in the center. Everyone else reaches out to lay a hand on the person in the center. All stand easy, focused on beaming trust and confidence to the center person, and wait for the "I'm ready" signal. When the person in the center lets go of the others' hands, that's the signal. When that happens, everyone steps back one pace. The person in the center falls, usually forward, and whoever's there in that part of the circle, usually two or three people, gently catch and return the faller to center. The faller falls again and again, falling in all directions and coming back to center. The faller stays stiff in the middle, so as to provide something to catch; the catchers work hard to communicate trust and confidence to the faller by the way they catch. No talking is permitted. After about 10 falls, catchers return the faller to rest; everyone reaches out again to touch the faller, who once again takes hands with two in the circle. The faller, eyes still closed, stands still until ready. When he or she releases the hands, everyone steps back, and the faller looks carefully at each person, turning around in the circle until everyone has made eye contact and wordlessly acknowledged what they just did. Many people find the eye contact harder than the falling. The faller then joins the circle and another steps in.

12. Jeffrey K. Liker et al., "Supplier Development in Product Development in Japan and the U.S." (University of Michigan working paper, Ann Arbor, Michigan, 1993).

13. It's vital to remember that throughout this essay, we're describing the theoretically best occasion of an ensemble in rehearsal. In practice, all these things are very hard to do, and mere humans often fall short of their ideals.

It's also essential to bear in mind that our discussions of actors' feelings, both as characters and as actors, are not meant to be sentimental and heartwarming. Actors use feeling and intellect as tools and methods; they're not alienated from them, as a line worker might be from an impact wrench, but they're not gooey about them, either.

Finally, there's a very good source of information and experience of actors and their working methods. James Lipton has conducted a series of interviews with notable actors, called *Inside the Actors' Studio*. These videos play and replay on Bravo. We strongly recommend them to anyone with a further interest in acting and Ensemble.

9 ARTFUL MAKING EMBRACES UNCERTAINTY INSTEAD OF PROTECTING AGAINST IT

Companies must often respond to unexpected events in the business environment. This is probably the most common reason they need to innovate. Unexpected events appear in many forms:

- A competitor suddenly cuts prices on products that compete with yours
- Materials arrive from a supplier in an unexpected size or shape, or at a time earlier or later than expected
- A customer places an unexpectedly large order
- A new product or process technology appears on the scene with potential to change the way your industry does business

These are just a few examples, but it should be clear in considering only these that all companies must deal with the unexpected, and must therefore innovate reliably in the course of everyday business. You may not think of your company as needing to be particularly innovative. Efficiency may seem more important. Maybe it is. But sooner or later, you'll need to innovate if only to improve ahead of your competitors.

From a process standpoint, innovation and efficiency *do* often seem to trade off. To maximize efficiency, companies often try to isolate making processes from *inessential* unexpected events, events that slow things down without signifying important changes or trends. For example, a company might find itself innovating (scrambling) every day because a supplier delivers materials late, in violation of the service agreement between the two companies. In such a case, the client company probably shouldn't change its making process before first insisting that the supplier address the problem. In other words, the company should try to *protect* its process from the uncertainty that calls for continual innovation instead of *changing* its process to accommodate the uncertainty. Protecting a making process against inessential uncertainty, as in this example, is a common and often successful strategy for companies. But it can be tricky to manage, as we can see through some examples.

McDonald's French Fries, Various Cattle, and Urgent Customer Orders

Fast food giant McDonald's protects itself from one kind of uncertainty by insisting that its suppliers provide raw French fries in precisely the right dimensions (width and depth).[1] Perfect conformance to this specification ensures that the fries will cook up properly in a mostly automated process executed by workers who have little or no discretionary control over their work. The company hires unskilled, low-wage people to watch over a carefully designed and strictly controlled replicating process. McDonald's replaces suppliers who can't conform to the specification. By protecting the process against uncertain inputs, McDonald's makes French fries quickly and efficiently, and customers get a consistent product.

Artful making embraces uncertainty, strives to be as attuned to it as possible.

Not everyone can so successfully protect key business processes against uncertain inputs. Management professor David Upton has written of a failed attempt at this kind of protection in the slaughter and processing of cattle.[2] The problem to be solved by cow processors differs from the McDonald's problem. Cows, the inputs of cow processing, come in many shapes and sizes. Unlike the frozen, pre-cut potato slices that are inputs to the McDonald's French-frying process, cows cannot be supplied in conformance to a specification of shape and size. In the case Upton describes, designers of cow-processing technology could not adequately predict the many permutations of cow shapes and sizes. Automatic equipment could not innovate when faced with novel inputs, so the system jammed a lot. Big problem. Messy.

Such difficulties have important parallels in other settings. In healthcare, for example, patients differ from each other, and their unexpected variations are *essential*, of their essence—they cannot be wished away for the sake of system efficiency.

Uncertainty in process inputs is only one of many categories of uncertainty that businesses face and that generate a need for innovation. Business professor David Garvin describes another type of problem faced by Digital Equipment in the 1980s.[3] No matter how hard Digital's managers tried to get their manufacturing plants operating in an orderly manner, customers simply would not cooperate. Customers loved Digital's products and kept asking for (and paying for!) more and more of them. Every time orderly manufacturing processes came within reach, another unexpected customer would appear with a huge, lucrative, urgent, and disruptive order. To meet the customers' needs, plant managers constantly expedited around their carefully designed processes, playing havoc with consistency and efficiency. To many in the plants, this escalating pattern seemed unsustainable, and it probably was. At the same time, financial markets were rewarding Digital for its ability to respond quickly to customer demands when other firms could not. The conclusion reached by some within the company, that Digital was doing something wrong by continually expediting around its orderly processes, seems perverse—they were satisfying their customers. An alternative and more interesting conclusion is that the orderly processes to which some of Digital's managers aspired were poorly suited to uncertain customer demand.[4]

ARTFUL MAKING DOESN'T PROTECT AGAINST UNCERTAINTY

Artful making embraces uncertainty, strives to be as attuned to it as possible. This may seem like a formula for chaos. When the need for order and efficiency exceeds the need for innovation and adaptability, or when uncertainties are mostly inessential, it probably is. As we've said, many business situations are unsuited to artful making.

But sometimes the variations experienced by companies *are* essential. Then a capacity to innovate is also essential. Artful making provides an approach to unexpected variation; it builds an ability to *improvise*, to incorporate and reconceive the unexpected into new and valuable outcomes. We revisit Hamlet and Ophelia for ideas about how to do this.

IMPROVISATION

In common usage, "to improvise" usually means to act without preparation.[5] Improvisation as a technique of artful making means something very different. Theatre improvisation presents a paradox: The more the actors have prepared for an improvisation, the more freedom they have, and the more creative outcomes they can generate.

Consider our rehearsals of *Hamlet*. George and Emily need to create the history of their relationship to guide their choices in rehearsal. To do this, they will improvise episodes in that history, inventing as they go along. Because this version of *Hamlet* is set in modern times (like the Ethan Hawke version set in a modern corporation instead of an ancient kingdom), they improvise a scene where Ophelia asks Hamlet over to watch TV. They start flirting, and this leads to kissing. Polonius interrupts to scold Ophelia and send Hamlet home. Shakespeare didn't write this scene, but the actors, in building their characters, need to know about all sorts of situations that Shakespeare didn't write.

Effective improvisation requires that no one ever refuses to accommodate the other's work. Each actor includes what the others do as a part of developing given circumstances. And, very important, everyone treats the improvisation, the doing of it, as an end in itself. That means that the actors follow their impulses wherever they lead. The actors don't edit their behavior to accommodate preconceived notions. No one ever says, "But my character wouldn't do that." What turns up in the improvisation may not fit in the play. The actors may create behavior that can't be unified with other important scenes. They may drop this improvisation and move on to something else. To an outsider this may seem like a failed experiment. It's not. If the actors act truthfully, the "failed" improvisation, though the audience will never notice it, will become part of the history between the two actors, and part of the play-to-be. The apparent failure is a vital step along the way.[6]

As they become more accustomed to surprises, actors become better at keeping themselves free of preconceptions. As they do, they become more capable of *reacting creatively to possibilities that were not envisioned in advance.*

Consider the action leading up to the moment Polonius happens into the room. Hamlet and Ophelia start off watching TV, but flirting turns to kissing. George and Emily know that Dennis (playing Polonius) is going to come in. How can they keep Hamlet and Ophelia from expecting him? How can they keep their expectation from inhibiting their actions? The director might intervene, might take Dennis aside and tell him, "Don't come in till I give you the signal." George and Emily notice that Dennis isn't appearing and begin to think the scene's been changed, that he's not coming in. Now they're in a fix. They begin to worry about what to do next, where all this kissing is going to end up if Dennis doesn't enter soon. When they've finally decided he's never going to appear, the director gives the sign: Polonius comes in and truly surprises George and Emily, and thus Hamlet and Ophelia.

Dennis has a similar problem. He knows what he's going to find. To help him, the director might tell him to wait in the hall so he doesn't see what's going on in the scene, then tell George and Emily to play cribbage instead of kissing. When Dennis gets the signal, he enters, expecting to be shocked and enraged, only to discover an innocent card game. His surprise, thus Polonius's, is genuine, his reaction unpredictable. The improvisation yields a fresh and stimulating action, full of new information the actors and director can use.

BUILDING IMPROVISATIONAL CAPABILITY: BEING IN "PRESENT TIME"

In each of these cases, the director has helped the actors by placing them in what we call "present time." As they become more and more accustomed to these kinds of surprises, actors become better and better at keeping themselves free of expectations and preconceptions. They become more capable of *reacting creatively to possibilities that were not envisioned in advance*. Dick Koos, in charge of simulation training for the Apollo moon landings, used similar tactics to prepare flight controllers for Apollo 11. As the team settled into comfortable routines, he would throw them simulation "curve balls" to bump loose their preconceptions, to keep them on their toes.[7] Businesses sometimes engage in "scenario thinking" to similar effect, working imaginatively through possibilities, avoiding preconceptions.

Too often, though, a business' goal-directed, industrial limitations degrade its ability to improvise, even in situations that desperately need it. In a recent visit to a large company, Rob saw a $125 million IT project that had become a disaster in exactly this way. In a project of such tremendous size (the largest single project of any kind ever attempted by the organization), unexpected complications in the system inevitably developed. The project was simply too complex for the engineers to envision all its difficulties in advance.

Nevertheless, the managers determined to fulfill expectations exactly, to keep everything precisely in line with plans. Ironically, it was the very high stakes of the project that made them think they couldn't tolerate potentially costly deviations.

The plans were set well before the project began, and the company's insistence on conformance to preconceived expectations stifled any efforts at midcourse correction. "Plan the work and work the plan" was their implicit mantra, and it led them directly to a costly and destructive course of action. Unexpected difficulties accumulated: Software didn't do everything it promised; organizational and process changes couldn't be completed as quickly or cheaply as planned. Managers discounted or ignored these difficulties because to acknowledge them would put the project off its planned schedule. Eventually, difficulties piled up and became impossible to ignore. By this time, the organization had little ability, and less willingness, to improvise in response to emerging difficulties. We'd all like to believe that this kind of problem is rare in business. It's not.

> Managers must give workers permission to invoke present time in preference to preconceived future times, to push back and say, "We need to be free of that expectation," no matter how high the stakes.

This large project disaster might not have happened had project team members been working in present time, reacting improvisationally to emerging given circumstances. Had they discussed problems as they arose, had their process made room for iterations that could create opportunities to reconceive both process and product, the schedule might not have been disrupted. Instead, the project team worked in "future time," creating for themselves a fictional time defined by detailed, preconceived (and, in the event, unattainable) expectations. There was no conversation and no attempt to reconceive the project until it had become a train wreck.

In situations conducive to artful making, a director/manager helps actors/workers stay at work in present time. This means throwing them a "curve ball" now and then. In Chapter 1, we saw that the director challenged actors in *Streetcar* by tinkering with their positions on stage. The actors, with their horseplay, also challenged the director and other actors. That's how this should go; think of the near mutiny and constant push-back against management at Sun. Managers must give workers permission to invoke present time in preference to preconceived future times, to push back and say, "We need to be free of that expectation," no matter how high the stakes.

Flexibility becomes more important as the stakes get higher. Workers, in turn, must understand that working in present time is part of the process, that the manager is not simply going out of the way to be difficult by throwing them a curve. As we've seen, part of getting this right involves making sure the workspace is safe enough that workers need not fear what will happen if they miss when they swing hard at a curve ball.

IMPROVISATION AND CONTROL

As we have seen, improvisation has a paradoxical center: The more thoroughly prepared you are, the more preparation and homework you've done, the more creative and unpredictable you can be. This idea harkens back to our discussion in Chapter 6 of control by release. What Lee observed in a recent visit with an accomplished painter is another version of the story in Chapter 6 of the designer, whose effortless chalk drawing on a huge piece of muslin demonstrated artful precision:

> Joy Mills got interested in Chinese watercolors. She took some classes, and began to paint. When I visited, she had been for some weeks working on iris in a vase. She showed me, not a painting of iris in a vase, but sheet after sheet of iris petals, hundreds of them, each one a single stroke of the brush, executed over and over and over. When she got to the actual picture, she would do it in a series of single strokes, every one needing to be perfect, because in the improvisatory Chinese manner, you only get one shot, no editing or fixing allowed. She grooved her stroke so she could improvise the painting.

The key to improvisation is preparation. Actors prepare for rehearsal and performance by inventing given circumstances, and by learning the lines of the script. They study both to the limits of their time, talent, and imagination. When they speak the playwright's lines, they must do so reflexively, without conscious thought, just as they do in an improvisation, just as

Joy must lay down each stroke of her painting. If what you're making is something new, something never seen before, your process must be an improvisation.

Impeccable preparation supports Release, the fundamental quality of artful making in rehearsal, the studio, or the meeting. If you know you've prepared impeccably, you can trust the truth and rightness of your impulsive, reflexive responses to what happens in the scene or in the meeting. You can trust them enough to impose your new gesture, your wild idea, on the others, giving them something they must include in their own work. If your impulse turns out to be incompatible with something else that's important (another character's action, a budget line), that's not a failure or defeat; it's a step along the way. You go back to your preparations, develop the given circumstances a bit differently, work the moment again (make another iteration), and come up with another impulsive, reflexive response, one that will again inject something new into the scene, meeting, or software.

ARTFUL MAKING AND INTERDEPENDENCY

Interventions that keep people on their toes have another advantage: They can trigger big, unexpected, valuable innovations. When actors or employees work to keep themselves free of preconceptions, apparently insubstantial interventions can have surprisingly beneficial ripple effects. At People's Light one day, Abigail Adams launched a production to an entirely new and higher level of excellence simply by suggesting that an actor walk the other way around the table. The suggestion had no apparent connection with the play's visible action. The direction around the table had no obvious relationship to the story, the dialogue, or the flow of the action at that moment. Adams thought of it as something that would affect the evolving visual tableau, a dimension of the play for which the actors on stage have little concern. To the actors,

> Because of built-in interdependencies, a small change necessitated many small adjustments, which moved forward from the change, conflicting and combining, to large effect.

the move was a change for them to cope with, something else to be absorbed into the work. But when they did it, the move led to other moves and countermoves, each prompting collaborative adjustments and inventions that, in combination, transformed the play.

Embedded within this story is an important principle: Artful innovation requires *interdependence* among makers, materials, forms, and even final purposes. An instruction to walk the other way around the table can't have the desired ripple effect if the process is designed so that individual actors do not affect each other. Because of built-in interdependencies, a small physical change necessitated many small adjustments, which moved forward from the change, conflicting and combining, to large effect. Artful makers cherish this kind of interdependency, just as they cherish uncertainty and ambiguity, accidents and "mistakes."

In business, we sometimes regard interdependencies as bad things. Often, in designing a product or process, we strive to insulate the parts from one another. The reasons we do this are pretty clear: If there are interdependencies between components of a product or process, then problems can have wide-ranging, unpredictable effects. For example, in designing an automobile, solving a problem in the electrical system might cause a problem in the cooling system. The problem that holds up the work of the electrical systems engineers then also holds up the work of the cooling systems engineers as they wait to see how the electrical problem gets resolved. Reducing interdependencies among components and systems—making product or process designs more *modular*—is an important strategy for protecting against uncertainty, for allowing work in parallel, and for managing complexity.[8] Modularity is an extremely useful concept when applied to a wide range of business settings.

How do we reconcile this apparent conflict between modular decoupling and artful making? Partly by noting that artful making *requires* some modularity in work process design. Modularity decouples work, so that people can work on manageable pieces of a problem, so they can work in parallel without working at cross purposes, and so that problems affecting one piece need not affect others. Artful makers often benefit from this kind of decoupling, especially when it helps establish a secure workspace (because things tried won't elicit criticism from beyond the workspace), and reduces the size and complexity of a task to make it a more suitable job for an ensemble.

Decoupling also has a critical effect on the cost of iteration. Exploration costs, part of the cost of iteration, can't be low if things tried that don't "work" have serious repercussions for customers or other teams of workers. Thus, a degree of modularity is required to maintain the low cost of iteration necessary for artful making. To ensure a low cost of iteration, iterations that don't "work" must be decoupled from others they might unacceptably affect.

It doesn't follow, though, that efforts to reduce and eliminate interdependencies should extend everywhere. Interdependencies within a module drive the artful innovation in that module. Interdependencies that reach *into* the making process from the outside often herald important changes in the environment that should also fuel innovation. In designing methodologies, artful makers should apply modularity to lower the iteration cost of work on various modules. But they should preserve interdependencies that lead to innovation within modules and remain open to interdependencies that reach *into* the ensemble. This principle of work design does not address all concerns about the tradeoffs between modularity and interdependency. Deciding where to draw lines between modules requires a sense of where—in what modules—innovation needs to emerge and has potential to emerge.

Modularity always has some dampening effect on artful activities. Setting up a modular product or process design requires planning. Designers and managers make choices in advance about which components and which subsystems get included in which modules. Such choices constitute commitments, for the time being at least, to a particular design framework. And designing out the interdependencies between modules eliminates triggers that might prompt artful reconsideration—reconceiving—of the framework. Difficulties in reacting to the appearance of "disruptive technologies"[9] can arise from a company's commitments to established architectures and from its inability to make innovative leaps to new architectures. The in-advance nature of architecture decisions, the fact that they create an architectural specification, means that artful iteration is less likely at an architectural level.

THE EMERGENT FINAL PURPOSE

Any made thing—play, or software version, or strategy—has a final purpose in the world. Some externally mandated conditions must be met: Armor must stop a bolt or blow; a minivan must safely transport a mom and five or six soccer players. It's a feature of an artfully made thing, however, that during the making process, these worldly purposes take a back seat to the integrity of the process itself. This is hard to think about—counterintuitive—but in a successfully undertaken artful making process, *we cannot head straight for the final purpose*. It must emerge from our work, from actions created in present time. We want to *preserve* the unpredictability of our results, not *protect* against it. We must be willing to set aside our plans for how the $125 million project should go to achieve a more valuable, unforeseen outcome.

You may be thinking, "Whoa!" Preserving the unpredictability of the results sounds like the last thing you want to do on a $125 million project. As we have seen, though, in the example of the large IT project that became a train wreck, our urge to make inherently unpredictable phenomena entirely predictable often leads to unhelpful project team behaviors, such as covering up unexpected problems or taking actions that used to be sensible but aren't anymore.

In a successfully undertaken artful making process, we cannot head straight for the final purpose. We must be willing to set aside our plans for how a project should go to achieve a more valuable, unforeseen outcome.

This observation doesn't answer all our concerns about the difficulty of managing inherently unpredictable processes. Indeed, how you finance artful making, how you manage the risks involved in paying for projects that do not, and in some cases cannot, have a well-defined objective is a critical issue.

Fortunately, it's not nearly as difficult an issue as it may at first appear. There are, in fact, many business precedents for dealing with such investments. In the next chapter, we will explain how to implement artful making and maintain fiscal responsibility.

ENDNOTES

1. David M. Upton and Joshua Margolis, "McDonald's Corporation" (Harvard Business School case no. 693-028, 1992).

2. David M. Upton, "The Cybertech Project (A)" (Harvard Business School case no. 695-030, 1995).

3. David A. Garvin and Janet Simpson, "Digital Equipment Corp.: The Endpoint Model (A)" (Harvard Business School case no. 688-059, 1988); David A. Garvin and Janet Simpson, "Digital Equipment Corp.: The Endpoint Model (B1)" (Harvard Business School case no. 688-060, 1988); David A. Garvin and Janet Simpson, "Digital Equipment Corp.: The Endpoint Model (B2)" (Harvard Business School case no. 688-061, 1988); David A. Garvin and Janet Simpson, "Digital Equipment Corp.: The Endpoint Model (C1)" (Harvard Business School case no. 688-062, 1988); and David A. Garvin and Janet Simpson, "Digital Equipment Corp.: The Endpoint Model (C2)" (Harvard Business School case no. 688-063, 1988).

4. Of course, uncertain customer demand is not the whole story here, either of Digital's eventual difficulties in the marketplace, or even of their difficulties in the Augusta, Maine plant (described in this case). In a supply chain such as the one Digital was trying to manage, there are complex "bullwhip" effects that accentuate the disruptions to the production system. Those needed to be managed also. Solving the problem is not merely a matter of building a flexible enough production system.

5. "To invent, compose, or recite without preparation," *The American Heritage Dictionary of the English Language*, New College Edition, William Morris, ed. (Boston: Houghton Mifflin Company, 1979) p. 662.

6. Again, we're describing the ideal case: highly skilled actors who have done their homework and who therefore trust their craziest impulses. Life pressures can degrade this ideal into reality, and a director/manager works to ease those pressures, or to accommodate them.

7. Gene Kranz, *Failure Is Not an Option: Mission Control from Mercury to Apollo 13 and Beyond* (New York: Simon and Schuster, 2000).

8. Carliss Baldwin and Kim Clark, "The Value and Consequences of Modularity in Design: A Summary of the Argument in *Design Rules 1*" (Harvard Business School working paper, March 14, 2002).

9. Clayton Christensen, *The Innovator's Dilemma* (Boston: Harvard Business School Press, 1998).

10 ARTFUL MAKING IS FISCALLY RESPONSIBLE

As the agile software development community knows, artful making in business can be controversial. Critics of artful processes see them as ad hoc, undisciplined, maybe even irresponsible. A dialogue recorded during a presentation by agile advocate Kent Beck illustrates a fairly common opinion that artful making in software development is a thinly veiled tactic for avoiding process rigor. The questioner here is responding to Beck's criticism of sequential software development methodologies, which have a separate and well-defined "design" phase:

Questioner: I'm worried about the fact that...you [agile software developers] don't do any design.

Beck: We do design for a couple of hours each day.

Questioner: That's what I'm concerned about—you don't do any design![1]

Beck and the questioner talk past one another. Beck says that his iterative approach includes design activities that occur during every iteration. The questioner refuses to call those activities "design" because they aren't carried out within a discrete and thorough period early in development called "the design phase." His skepticism makes perfect sense in situations that require a sequential, planning-intensive approach.

People trained to fear inadequate planning and lack of accountability often react immediately, viscerally, and negatively to artful making.

While we believe in the value of artful making when the prerequisite conditions are satisfied, we recognize serious questions, especially about budgeting and fiscal responsibility. It's all very well to let your artful makers run out of control sometimes, but at what point does that become an irresponsible use of shareholder-owned resources? And, perhaps even more problematic: How do you budget for an artful making process? How do you know how much it's going to cost? Fortunately, there are good answers to these questions, based in familiar business situations with similar characteristics.

People trained to fear inadequate planning and lack of accountability often react immediately, viscerally, and negatively to artful making.

DEADLINES AND RELIABLE INNOVATION

We've seen that in rehearsal, iterative, emergent innovation is not inconsistent with firm deadlines. And that's the first-order answer to questions about how long a manager should let a team run "out of control." As long as letting the team run continues to produce valuable innovation *on time* and *within budget*, you have a strong case for control by release. A team working artfully often has a track record that can help you make decisions about letting the team alone. Since you can't really monitor such a group very well, you're sort of at its mercy anyway.

Reliably meeting deadlines helps with the question about how you budget for artful making. Like industrial making, artful making usually requires a certain amount of up-front technology investment. In artful making, we aim that investment at cheap and rapid iteration, not at an efficient replication process. That up-front investment is largely a fixed cost, and for a lot of knowledge work, it's not particularly high. Software developers, for example, need a system that permits rapid builds, a version control system (to assure that you can rewind from things you try that don't "work"), and a disciplined system for testing and migrating changes into released products (so that the things you try that don't "work" don't impose unacceptably high costs on customers). Even non-agile development environments usually include these components, so the incremental costs of setting up an infrastructure to support cheap and rapid iteration aren't high. Once the infrastructure is in place, we can use it for many different projects and products.

The variable costs associated with artful making are mostly people costs, which are relatively easy to manage when you insist on a reliable deadline. Number of people, multiplied by time until deadline, multiplied by average wages, gives you a pretty good cut at a budget.[2] In this model, you have only one variable left: How many developmental iterations can we fit into the available time? The number of iterations has a direct impact on the *scope* of the project—in software development, the number of features the product can include. As the deadline approaches, developers may drop some lower priority features. In more traditional approaches, management fixes and insists on a required feature set. Variation, if any, shows up in a pushed-back deadline.

However, reliable innovation under deadline does not completely allay reasonable concerns about artful making budgets. Some business situations allow for little variation in the scope of what's accomplished. Often, core requirements must be met, none of which can be omitted. The budgeting problem then becomes a question of how much it will cost and how long it will take to build a good enough system that includes all required features. Fortunately, there's a business precedent for financing emergent projects and enterprises in an iterative manner when hard requirements must be met: venture capital financing. To budget successfully when the project aims at general results (e.g., business success) rather than detailed, preconceived outcomes, when at any moment unexpected complications may appear or artful methods may create startling new directions for thought and work, managers with budget responsibility must let go of their preconceived notions and learn to think like venture investors.

FUNDING EMERGENT PROJECTS:
A VENTURE-BASED APPROACH[3]

The challenges faced by professional venture investors have elements in common with those of a financial manager trying to plan for an artful making project. In both cases, the

When it comes to innovation, business budgeters must learn to think a little more like venture investors.

products, services, and capabilities that result from the project (venture) are not fixed; they emerge over time. Both require innovation, creating entirely anew. Planning is difficult in their ambiguous circumstances, and there's plenty of midcourse adjustment.

The task at hand for both venture investor and artful budgeter is to deploy finite resources across a portfolio of investments and to manage those investments to produce the highest possible return. A diagram (Figure 10–1) developed by HBS professor Bill Sahlman, an expert on the venture capital (VC) industry, provides us with a frame of reference.[4] Any new venture contains some probability that the investment will be written off completely. In a business project, this happens when the project is abandoned before producing any tangible benefit. The spike above the -100% return in the diagram represents this possibility. The probability of various rates of return greater than -100% spreads out in a distribution represented by the bell curve in the figure. An investor managing such an initiative has two goals: (1) to reduce the height of the -100% spike (that is, the probability of a total write-off); and (2) to move the distribution of returns to the right, increasing the probability of higher returns. Venture financiers manage their investments in numerous ways to achieve these goals, but we'll follow Sahlman's example and focus on three factors: staging, risk sharing, and people.

STAGING

Sahlman describes how professional investors *stage* their investments in an emergent venture:

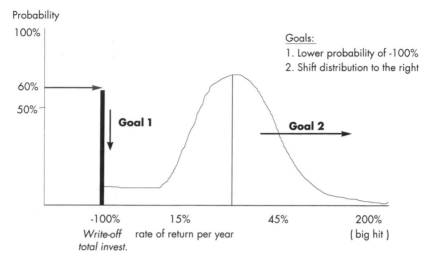

FIGURE 10–1
Sahlman's model of the venture investment challenge.

> If a company believes it needs $10 million to develop and introduce a software product, they are likely to find that no investor will invest the full $10 million. Rather, the investor will stage the commitment of capital over time, preserving the right to invest more money and preserving the right to abandon the project . . . The issue of how much money to invest . . . is exceedingly difficult and the perspectives of the players often differ . . . investors want to stage the capital over time in order to "buy" information.[5]

This is a financial version of artful making. It's iterative, and it explicitly incorporates the need to reconceive the venture as it progresses. It means funding the project in increments, with frequent reconceiving points. With proper management, the need to come back later for more funding will serve as a trigger for reconceiving. This model of venture funding and artful making fit together extremely well. Given that new ventures are all about innovation, this is, of course, far from coincidental.

A management team accustomed to traditional budgeting processes may find it hard to think this way. An incremental investment model is more interactive, more organic than a static budget. Conventional budgeters tend to think of all projects as standard capital investment, more like buying equipment than funding a new venture. They insist on full quantification of costs and benefits at the start. But the uncertainty that generates a need for artful making means that expenditures on such projects *must* be staged so as to buy information about the right combinations of people, strategy, and tactics. An artfully made product may not look much like the original concept. Lock in too rigidly with original conceptions and you risk dysfunctional outcomes—outcomes that don't meet your evolving business need, or business solutions with serious but concealed flaws—just as surely as rigidity in the theatre produces wooden, lifeless plays.[6]

The venture investor's approach is a financial version of artful making. It's iterative, and it explicitly incorporates the need to reconceive the venture as it progresses.

Staging can be used to introduce artful methods into situations where they might not seem applicable on first glance. For example, when Tektronix implemented a huge commercial enterprise software system, they subdivided the overall initiative into roughly 20 "waves." Each wave delivered a set of functionality for a division or geographic region. The first wave delivered integrated financials (minus accounts receivable) for all three of the company's divisions, but only in the U.S. When company managers began implementing functionality outside the U.S., they scaled down the size of the waves to reflect the greater risk of unanticipated problems. Only after project managers had incorporated learning from earlier waves into the emerging project, and after pilot installations had proved successful, did they begin a general rollout in Europe. As one implementation team member noted, their intention to buy information was explicit: "We decided to plan incrementally, and roll out future waves as we learned more about the process." Cisco Systems, in a similarly successful enterprise software installation, used an approach they called "rapid, iterative prototyping," which had many of these same features.[7]

INCENTIVE ALIGNMENT AND RISK SHARING

Venture investors have evolved a sophisticated set of financial practices to produce incentive alignment among the parties involved in a new venture. Investors want to assure that their own losses on the venture will be felt by the decision-makers (the entrepreneurs) so that everyone strives for the same goals. Investors make sure incentives are aligned by writing formal contracts that reward the management team only when investors realize concrete rewards. They make sure everyone has "skin in the game." As we have seen, goal alignment in artful making is very important, but trickier than simply writing contracts.

It's possible to get too cute with financial incentives, to produce incentives that have complex, unintended effects, such as encouraging people to play accounting games (plenty of examples of this have made headlines in recent years). Moreover, innovative knowledge work involves problem-solving and creative activities that inherently interest workers. This produces motivations too complex to be well-managed on a purely financial basis. Knowledge workers tend to think of themselves as professionals who obtain personal reward from their work. They need financial reward to feel that their contributions are appreciated, and they need to perceive fairness in financial arrangements. But getting everyone to have skin in the game is rarely a financial matter in artful making. Ensemble members believe in their relationships and in the intrinsic value of their work; that belief is their skin, and to them it is the game.

At one point in the Tektronix implementation, managers decided to shift away from incentive payments toward a time-and-materials basis. Their teams established strong trust-based relationships and financial incentives became distracting. Their teams had become ensembles and the skin they had in the game meant more than money.

Artful managers do well to think of keeping everyone's incentives aligned in a participative manner. A manager/director can influence focus and instill a sense of mission in the group. A compelling group effort toward ensemble-based results does

It's possible to get too cute with financial incentives, to produce incentives that have complex, unintended effects.

more good than a detailed financial goal. "Produce a significant piece of collaborative art"; "Do good for our patients"; "Make a successful business": These sentiments dovetail with knowledge workers' sense of their collective purpose and thus align incentives for artful makers much better than too-cute financial arrangements.

"PEOPLE, PEOPLE, PEOPLE!"

Venture financing methods and artful making have another close parallel: They both assume that people are the most important factor in assuring successful outcomes. The first consideration of venture investors as they evaluate a business proposal is the team. There's an old adage: "I'd rather back an 'A' team with a 'B' idea than a 'B' team with an 'A' idea." This raises an issue that we haven't discussed yet, but which is of central importance to artful making: *casting*.

In a theatre, casting is the most important set of choices a director makes. Everything follows from casting. Using the word in a business context reminds us that we're not talking about interchangeable full-time equivalents (FTEs) or units of labor, but rather individual persons with specific characteristics and powers more or less suited to particular roles. Although managers appreciate the importance of choosing the "right person for the job," the lens of theatre is more sophisticated than the ones we often use in business.

It's obvious that Dustin Hoffman and Sigourney Weaver are not interchangeable units of labor. They aren't suited to play the same part. But it's not uncommon for managers to discuss project staffing in language that implies just such interchangeability. As Tom DeMarco and Tim Lister note in their book, *Peopleware*, managers sometimes behave "as though there were a magical People Store they could call up and say, 'Send me a new George Gardenhyer, but make him a little less uppity.'"[8] Fred Brooks, in *The Mythical Man-Month*, points out the folly of thinking this way on software development projects, and his observations apply to all artful making.[9] Adding people to a late project, Brooks maintains, makes it later. Why? Because adding new people into the interdependent mix of a team doing complex knowledge work not only forces a complete redefinition of roles and group dynamics, it also takes up time while the group absorbs and gets to know the new people. A second Willy Loman added to the cast won't make a better *Death of a Salesman*, nor will it speed up rehearsals.

It's also clear that no matter how good you get at repeating (not replicating!) a play, you can't replace Dustin Hoffman or Sigourney Weaver with a less expensive beginner and expect to maintain quality. The industrial making strategy of routinizing process, protecting it from uncertainty, and then substituting lower cost labor doesn't work. Industrial making incentive and compliance mechanisms that usually accompany this strategy also work badly here. Many managers understand this, but even so, business organizations are full of incentive mechanisms that encourage people to work harder rather than smarter. Such methods interfere with artful making by framing the value of work at the individual level, thereby placing the interests of individuals in conflict and removing the quality of Ensemble from the team.

Although the skills and characteristics of actors do influence casting decisions, we should keep in mind that there's a theoretically infinite number of ways to cast any part. As we have seen, Shakespeare had Richard Burbage, a tall, slightly fat actor (who also owned the company) in mind for Hamlet. No Hamlet since, until Simon Russell Beale, has been anything but sleek and handsome (think Mel Gibson). But anything's possible. Even a few women have played the part to effect.[10]

> In artful making, it's convenient to think of selection decisions as "casting." Casting choices are Interdependent. A director/manager chooses among combinations, not individuals.

But casting a woman as Hamlet must influence other choices as well. Casting is not a matter of "finding the right person for the job"—not exactly. Casting means selecting a cast capable of mounting the play; though each actor could play the part well, casting six-foot-tall Janet McTeer as Ophelia opposite not-quite-six-foot-tall Tom Cruise as Hamlet would create unnecessary difficulties. The parts of an ensemble are not inter-changeable; casting choices are interdependent. Indeed, an actor seeking a role will often be asked to read the part with a number of other actors, so that the director can choose among combinations, not individuals. Gene Kranz reports that team member interdependencies were prominent in the minds of those who made mission-control staffing decisions: "The branch chiefs carefully matched the personalities and strengths of controllers to those of the individual flight directors."[11]

FISCAL RESPONSIBILITY IN ARTFUL MAKING

Most business people rarely think about management in arts organizations. When they do, it's often with a degree of condescension, an implicit assumption that business thinking is far advanced over the arts in most important management dimensions. The belief in business that arts organizations aren't fiscally well-managed shows up regularly in places like grant applications, which often enforce a businesslike, restraint-based approach to organizational control as a prerequisite for a contribution to the arts organization. Just as we have raised in this book the possibility that business people can learn a lot from artists about innovation, we now suggest that some arts organizations do quite well when it comes to fiscal perform-ance; they do better, in fact, than many businesses.

People's Light has finished 27 of its last 28 seasons "in the black." In the year they went over budget, they made a delib-erate decision, a successful investment in building the capabil-ities of the institution by professionalizing the staff. How many businesses have done as well for as long? A program officer at a foundation once called People's Light a "$7 million operation running on a $3 million budget."[12] How many businesses get so much bang for their buck? It's time to take a reflective look at our assumptions in this area. Not only is artful making a good fit with fiscal responsibility, it offers a progressive model of what fiscal responsibility can mean.

ENDNOTES

1. James A. Highsmith III, *Agile Software Development: Principles, Practices, and Ecosystems* (Boston: Addison-Wesley, 2002) p. 45.

2. It's possible, of course, to impose a deadline that is simply unachievable. Artificial compression of development schedules is a commonly attempted strategy for reducing cost and shortening schedules, but it is a thoroughly discredited strategy that rarely works and has no place in artful making.

3. Robert D. Austin and Richard L. Nolan, "Manage ERP Initiatives as New Ventures, Not IT Projects" (Harvard Business School working paper no. 99-024, 1998).

4. William A. Sahlman, "How to Write a Great Business Plan," *Harvard Business Review* (July–August 1997) p. 98.

5. Sahlman.

6. Dorothy A. Leonard-Barton, *Wellsprings of Knowledge: Building and Sustaining the Sources of Innovation* (Boston: Harvard Business School Press, 1995).

7. For more information on these implementation projects, see Robert D. Austin, Richard L. Nolan, and Mark J. Cotteleer, "Cisco Systems, Inc.: Implementing ERP" (Harvard Business School case no. 699-022, 1999); and Robert D. Austin, Richard L. Nolan, Mark J. Cotteleer, and George Westerman, "Tektronix, Inc.: Global ERP Implementation" (Harvard Business School case no. 699-043, 1999).

8. Tom DeMarco and Timothy Lister, *Peopleware: Productive Projects and Teams*, 2nd edition (New York: Dorset House Publishing, 1999) p. 9.

9. Fredrick P. Brooks, *The Mythical Man-Month, Anniversary Edition: Essays on Software Engineering* (Boston: Addison-Wesley, 1995).

10. Sarah Bernhardt, in her sixties, and with one leg lost to amputation, was the most famous.

11. Gene Kranz, *Failure Is Not an Option: Mission Control from Mercury to Apollo 13 and Beyond* (New York: Simon and Schuster, 2000) p. 258.

12. Robert D. Austin, "The People's Light and Theatre Company" (Harvard Business School case no. 600-055, 2000).

11 ARTFUL MANAGEMENT

Artful managers begin a project with some ideas of the outcomes they desire, but without controlling preconceptions. They set up a low-cost, iterative process that facilitates exploratory production. They coach their performers on a journey that they themselves cannot take, using earned trust to influence the focus of the group. They believe that good ideas will emerge from an impeccable process, and they moderate a complex, multi-layered interaction in which many elements converge over time, though they never lock in on exact replication. Artful processes elicit innovation in every iteration, hence they are never perfectly consistent. They are, nevertheless, reliable and precise when it comes to the requirements that must be met.

An artful manager's job isn't easy. It requires an appreciation for the characteristics and capabilities of each unique ensemble and each unique ensemble member. It requires subtlety, authority, and above all, patience. Artful management can't, therefore, be distilled into a five-step "how-to" program. It *is* possible, though, as we come to the end of this book, to underline some practical lessons and essential themes.

MANAGING CONVERGENCE AND EMERGENCE

A play's director manages the *convergence* of vague ideas into less vague ideas, of available materials into an emerging form. The rate of convergence is a primary concern. As the play-to-be moves toward performance, it inevitably takes on greater regularity, a persistent, increasingly recognizable shape. The actions of the emerging play become more and more similar from iteration to iteration. If this happens too quickly, the ensemble fails to explore the space of possibilities adequately; if it happens too slowly, the play won't be ready for opening night.

Almost always, managing the rate at which the form of a play emerges from the chaos of individual preparations involves some coordination of artful and industrial making methods. As we have seen, few activities can be considered pure artful making, play making included. Long before rehearsals start, designers begin their work. Since they make physical things, they must plan and schedule, then follow through. They make their plans and provisions early on; they change them rarely, at great expense and difficulty. One of a director's most pressing duties is to manage the development and completion of these designs, to orchestrate the introduction of these more industrially made elements into the artful making work of the actors, so that in their progress they help rather than hinder each other.

> A play's director manages the convergence of vague ideas into less vague ideas, of available materials into an emerging form. The rate of convergence is a primary concern.

The activities of a wise manager in charge of a project team that doesn't or can't have a well-formed idea of its specific outcome need not be much different from those of a theatre director. A manager supervising the creation of a new strategy at a technology company will facilitate employees' work, create unity among the various parts of the ongoing work, manage the rate at which the ensemble makes its choices, and articulate the form of the strategy as it begins to assume a shape. This manager, aware that every part of this process must influence every other, will continue to arrange things so that the emerging parts will help and not hinder each other. Most strategy-makers will be doing knowledge work, but physical work constraints may need consideration: Implacable physical lead times, for example. The manager brings the work and materials together and reconceives them repeatedly so that the final product emerges out of everyone's effort. The alternative, arranging it all toward a preconceived product, while possible in some cases, won't be as interesting for the makers; worse, it will lead to a less effective strategy from a less capable team.

About a week before a play's opening, the production team adds all the technical accompaniments (lights, sound, costumes, etc.) and the play-to-be assumes its (never quite final) shape. The director takes the lead in identifying choices that will persist. In the best work of this kind, the right choice seems inevitable. It is the choice that must be made for the next set of choices to appear. As opening night nears, the range of improvisational choices narrows: If you've been delivering that climactic line from stage left, there will come a time when you may no longer choose to try it from stage right. Part of the director's job is to know when that time has come. The entire process moves in fits and starts from development toward repetition (*not* replication!), as everyone learns to run the always-new play by repeating it over and over.

After opening night, the actors, playing each moment as if for the first time, create subtle though significant differences in each performance: They continually develop and improve the work throughout the run. But the emergent process is highly reliable, and rigorous. We've noted that a two-hour play typically finishes within 30 seconds of the same time every night. Within that range lies infinite variety. The actors come to work a day older, there's a brand new audience, and together they create something new every time.

ESSENTIAL THEMES

Three essential themes arise from our study of artful making:

1. Successfully getting reliable innovation from knowledge workers requires a diligent faith in an impeccable process, knowing that it will produce something of value before a firm deadline.

2. Managing knowledge workers calls for collaboration without detailed or coercive direction, keeping in mind that you can't supervise talented employees in any conventional sense; you must lead them with passionate support and faith in their work.

3. Innovation in knowledge work requires de-stigmatizing "mistakes" and "failures," celebrating them as steps on the path to innovation. Remember, it's the first eight bench presses that turn the ninth into progress. In artful making, you can't skip to the end.

None of these themes is earth-shattering. Similar recommendations appear elsewhere in the management literature. But all three themes are, implicitly or explicitly, in conflict with some common business practices and some credible management scholarship. The example and metaphor of collaborative theatre art provide needed reinforcement of these themes, and a coherent framework within which we can think creatively about them.

Artful making, which we propose as a reliable approach to knowledge work innovation, resembles night vision. Say you're looking in the backyard for your black Labrador, Hannah. But she's invisible, the same color as the night. You might catch a glimpse of her over by the hedge. If you focus just to one side of where you think she is, she'll appear out of the dark. Look right at her, though, and she's gone. The night vision metaphor applies to almost every aspect of artful making. At first, everyone has a professional but vague idea of where they'll end up. But if anyone focuses on achieving exactly this beginning idea, his or her work (and consequently, everyone else's work) will suffer.

ARTFUL MANAGEMENT SIGNPOSTS

We've mentioned that Toyota has long permitted executives from other companies to tour its plants, to see its famous production system in action, without much fear that they will usefully copy the system. They know that the tendency in business is to take the easy way—to copy the surface features of a method and proclaim success, rather than do the hard work of real mastery. Indeed, few outside Toyota have mastered the Toyota Production System.

A similar principle applies to artful making. You won't succeed at it by making the easy choice, or by converting it into terms with which you are already familiar and comfortable. What artists do is not just an inferior form of what business people do, even when it comes to pursuing the objectives of business. You won't command, incentivize, or optimize an ensemble into being.

One of a director's most pressing duties is to orchestrate the introduction of industrially made elements into the artful making work, so that each helps rather than hinders the other.

Although we provide the following eight points of advice, we urge you not to consider these all there is to artful making. Artful making is a process, and as such, it can truly be known only in the doing. These eight points are signposts, worth keeping in mind on your journey. Each of these points of advice corresponds to one or more earlier chapters.

1. *Emergence*—Nurture and trust emergence. Don't try to "get it right the first time." Instead, create a team and a process that can "make it good before the deadline" (Chapter 2).

2. *Iteration*—Build iteration into your processes. Iteration creates and defines the problem as a way of searching for valuable outcomes. Think of iteration as *making* rather than *discovering* (Chapter 3).

3. *Prerequisites*—Use artful and industrial making in conditions appropriate to each. Don't overestimate the usefulness of artful making. Don't underestimate it, either. Apply technology to reduce the cost of iteration

rather than to automate processes end-to-end. Focus on cheap and rapid iteration in the making process, not on the efficiency of the process as you conceive it today (Chapters 4 and 5).

4. *Control*—Accept that you can't conventionally supervise your employees anymore. Teach them to release, and release them. You don't take the journey with them. Emphasize "mechanics," not compliance mechanisms (Chapter 6).

5. *Improvising, reconceiving, collaborating*—Build the ability of your teams and organization to improvise, to reconceive constraints and complications into new opportunities. Keep in mind the differences between replicating and reconceiving. Don't try to turn development into a factory. Ditto for strategy making, or anything else that requires steering when you can't know your destination in advance. Seek collaboration and avoid the compromises that impair the coherence and integrity of what you're making (Chapter 7).

6. *Workspace*—Secure it. As you throw your team curve balls, make it safe for them to swing without restraint. Refrain from threats and punitive exercises of power. Be accessible. Honor limitations. Earn the trust and respect of the ensemble by trusting and respecting them. Support your people in their work on the edge (Chapter 8).

7. *Uncertainty*—Embrace it. Don't protect against it. Let it drive the reconceiving process. Practice your ability to work without preconception, to improvise. Throw your team curve balls; make them walk the other way around the table. Isolate the impacts of their exploration from customers and others in the organization, but don't design away all process interdependencies (they are your major source of innovation). Make processes and products modular enough to work, but not too modular for collaboration (Chapter 9).

8. *Fiscal responsibility*—Insist on it. Creative freedom depends on it. Finance artful making incrementally. Buy information about what it takes to succeed. Make

sure everyone strives toward the same refinement of process. Cast your project very carefully. Casting is the most important factor in determining success (Chapter 10).

THE ARTFUL MAKING QUALITIES

Anything new, observed W. Edwards Deming (among many others), at first appears to lack form. He argued that we need a "theory," a way of organizing our thoughts about a new thing, before we can *know* anything about it. Alternative theories provide different views into the same problem, and some views are more useful in a particular context than others. Deming's theory about uncanny systems gave him a way to think in new categories about problems within factories. It turned out to be more useful than older theories for many old and new problems.

The activities we've called knowledge work, some of them quite new to business, some of ancient origin, also need a "theory" to help managers and workers to think about them. Our usual categories for thinking about work, developed to understand industrial work in factories, are, we have argued, inadequate for gaining a deep understanding of knowledge work, particularly its innovative aspects. In this book, we've proposed the collaborative art of theatre, and particularly rehearsal, as an enabling metaphor—a theory, as Deming used that word—for thinking about new kinds of work. In this section, we offer a simple framework that summarizes the artful approach as viewed through an artful lens, the qualities of artful making:

Release

Collaboration

Ensemble

Play

It's important to realize that these qualities, and our description of how they interrelate, are really only ways of looking at things we've already seen in other ways. Viewing innovation through a business lens, we see iterative structure, prerequisite cost conditions, kinds of control, teamwork, uncertainty, and product. But those are not the categories artists choose for themselves. Having come this far in our story, we can now turn the knob on our conceptual microscope so that the business categories move into the background and the artists' categories move into sharp focus in the foreground. We do this to consider the activities of artists *in their own terms*. As we mentioned in the Introduction, it was our experience during this project that we missed the point artists were trying to make when we insisted on translating their ideas into management concepts already familiar and comfortable to us. Furthermore, it just makes sense to consider how these most reliable of under-time-pressure innovators think about what they do.

THE FOUR QUALITIES

We've illuminated the four qualities by describing rehearsal and other artful activities, including some in business. We call these qualities, not parts, because each manifests throughout the work, in every moment. We can extract them from the work only conceptually. Work that doesn't have all these qualities throughout isn't artful making.

Qualities are not the same as parts. If a person is courageous, then the quality of courage pervades that person. It does not reside in a particular part of them, and it can't be lopped off.

To think of work in this way, as having these four qualities, allows you to reconceive much of what you do along artful lines. To aid this process, we gather up and review the qualities and their interdependence.

RELEASE

Release at first seems to be the opposite of control. It's not. It's a form of control, the first quality of artful making. Control by release requires careful preparation that aims behavior rather than restrains it. Released behavior, like the acting teacher's pen, achieves a desired action but in unpredictable ways, as it follows the "gravity" created by the ensemble.

Release allows artful makers to move past tensions and inhibitions to gain access to original ideas and outrageous thoughts. For managers and business team members, release moves a person beyond vanity toward a new willingness to express strange, new ideas, to collaborate freely and thus discover a new range of responses to the work of others in the ensemble. When mastered, Release allows workers to reach their edges, to experience without mental or emotional complications the discomfort of an edge caused by tension, to practice on an edge, to discriminate between edge discomfort and injury pain. Inseparable from the ability to release into work on the edge is the skill of focus, which provides artful makers with a means to direct their attention productively, regardless of inevitable distractions. When performers achieve the quality of Release in all aspects of their working together, they collaborate.

COLLABORATION

Collaboration is a *conversation* that arises out of individual release, from which all parties come away with new ideas. The basic technique of Collaboration is reconceiving. Reconceiving in artful making replaces the industrial technique of replication, and the political technique of compromise. Collaborators reconceive a problem or process in light of each other's contributions, using them as material out of which, in combination with their own ideas, they make new, unpredictable ideas. When artful makers collaborate, either on a play production or a business plan, they contribute to the making of something else as well, something larger than the sum of the individual makers: an ensemble.

ENSEMBLE

The word "ensemble" does double duty as both a name and a quality. An ensemble at work on a project is a group that exhibits the quality of Ensemble. This kind of tautology is characteristic of art; it accounts for some of the difficulty the industrial-minded have in grasping the principles of art or of artful making. People working collaboratively, in the kind of secure workspace we've described, create an entity playmakers call an ensemble. This group differs in many ways from a conventional team. It exhibits the quality of Ensemble, which we've described. The most important single feature of an ensemble is that it, and the made thing it creates, are larger and more interesting than any one in it: It's greater than the sum of its parts.

Consider the Toyota Production System. When a worker stops the line and the team leader and others converge to help solve the problem, the group must be prepared to address predictable problems, and also to improvise solutions to problems no one has foreseen. If the team is well cast and has worked together for a while, they will work as an ensemble and be capable of amazing things. Their collaboration becomes, in the moment, an end in itself. When the problem is solved, the team will disperse. But for the duration of their work together, they create a situation in which the work and the thing they make, the fix, become one. We can imagine them going back to their usual tasks almost reluctantly, waiting for the next problem, ready for the improvisation, the most interesting and important part of their job. At Toyota or anywhere else, Ensemble doesn't appear magically as a result of sentimental incantation. It's the hard-won result of Collaboration, born of the practice that enables Release. We've called the product made by an ensemble a "play."

PLAY

In the theatre, plays are characterized by the fact that they exist only while they are being made. The act of making a play *is* the play. We have argued (as have others) that this is increasingly true of business products too; that the product of a business should be redefined as the experience of its interaction with customers, an interaction in which both product and customers vary over time. We've remarked how the product in car making has changed, from a physical thing to the totality of interaction between the automaker and the customer, possibly extending over the life of many individual cars. "Play" denotes an experience for customers and the act of making that experience. The ensemble member on the Toyota line plays in this sense. He or she is part of the making, and part of the total experience of the customer—part of the play.

If the product and the process of making are the same, it follows that attention to the process is the most important aspect of making. An impeccable process will yield a valuable product. This emphasis on process clarifies the artful making shift away from rigid plans and prescribed goals, toward deep preparation and improvised collaboration. The product of an artful making process develops during that process. It's a result, not a goal.

RELATIONSHIPS AMONG QUALITIES

These four qualities, interdependent with each other, give conceptual form to apparently formless complex processes. Release operates to create new and original action. Actions combine in Collaboration, as individuals work together to reconceive old into new. When Collaboration flourishes with skilled workers in a secured workspace, it yields a new creation, Ensemble. Out of Ensemble emerges Play, the form on which action converges, but which never locks in on perfect repetition. Or, to express the relationships in reverse: Play emerges from Ensemble, which results from Collaboration, which needs Release.

Each of the activities and concepts brought into focus by the various lenses of the artful making "theory" can be used to analyze, interpret, and improve your unique tasks and methods. The qualities provide a frame for any set of facts; they can be of significant benefit as you work to organize your facts and conceive the form of your particular situation. They are an alternative way to conceive knowledge work, a frame to replace the industrial thinking that conceives work in categories appropriate to factories.

A Director on Management

Abigail Adams is not only the senior director of People's Light and Theatre Company, she is also the CEO, though she doesn't use that title. As CEO, she is responsible for management tasks like those of any business. Her approach to directing guides her understanding of her business duties:

There's tremendous overlap between managing and directing. It makes perfect sense to me that what I am doing when I am "administering" is really very similar to what I'm doing in the rehearsal room. You get as many people as possible understanding what it is you're doing together. You make sure everyone understands the larger picture. At the same time, you make sure that their autonomy is safeguarded, that they can work in ways that will be supportive and challenging. My management style is throwing out questions. And I do exactly that same thing as a director. I think a lot of people have the idea that directors mostly give instructions, and certainly some directors do that. But even directors that do very tight staging and choreography—if they are any good—are able to adjust because the actor brings them an idea that they hadn't thought of.[1]

The things you are able to plan are those things you see as being possible. Impossibilities never make it to the planning stage.

The advantage in this management style is that it makes new things possible that can't be produced under more directive, industrial styles. Aisha Hobbes, one of Adams's younger employees, puts it this way:

Making the impossible possible, even in the arena of make-believe or pretend, does something to your brain. It allows you to envision—not plan—that's completely different. Planning is an activity that involves weighing pros and cons, taking into consideration available resources, and coming up with a strategy to achieve your goals. The things you are able to plan are those things you see as being possible. Impossibilities never make it to the planning stage. Whereas *envisioning* involves faith in a maybe and a belief in the chance that the *maybe* can become a *yes*.[2]

If we see these two views of work through the lens of artful making, using the qualities to think with, and rehearsal, with its cheap and rapid iteration, as our enabling metaphor, we're in position to do creative work, to make things never before seen, predicted, or even dreamed.

ENDNOTES

1. Robert D. Austin, "The People's Light and Theatre Company" (Harvard Business School case no. 600-055, 2000).

2. Ibid.

A FINAL WORD

12

In the 1990s, a remarkable software product emerged onto the corporate computing landscape and met with surprising acceptance. The product arose, not from a known and trusted company, but from a loosely affiliated army of programmers coordinating their work across the Internet. Remarkably, they all worked on the project *without pay*.

We refer, of course, to the Linux operating system, which continues to pose a serious threat to some of behemoth Microsoft's favorite money products. Linux has achieved a high degree of penetration into corporate markets, and is widely viewed as more reliable and secure than equivalent products from the world's best software companies.

As far as we know, in the actual creation of Linux no company made a profit. No person got rich. And yet, the product itself is superb. For a time, there were university seminars full of economists and business researchers desperate to explain the phenomenon as a result of self-interest and business incentives, urgently uncomfortable with the question, "Why did this work?"

The motives of the thousands of creators of Linux probably were not purely altruistic. Many harbored explicit antagonism toward Microsoft and longed to remove the company from its position at the top of the technology company heap. Others probably cared about their own reputations, fame within a community of peers whose opinions they respected. Maybe some even thought, as some economists have hypothesized, they would get great jobs as a result of the work they did on Linux. Despite all of these possibilities, there's a persistent sense that an awful lot of work got done on Linux without any conventional business motives. The group that created Linux wasn't exactly an ensemble, but they were, we believe, involved in their work for some of the same reasons: because they liked the work; because they thought what they were making was way cool.

Such motives appear in business every day. All across the world there are consultants, designers, managers, marketers, programmers, surgeons, testers, and other makers of all kinds motivated by their involvement in the work, for whom financial considerations and conventional business motives are not the most important thing. This kind of motivation is essential to artful making. It can be nurtured by managers, and can result in reliable, on-time innovation and highly profitable business.

Artful makers need a source of energy to fuel their confidence and give them courage to strike out into the unknown territory of the new. There are two main sources of this energy: good managers and personal vocation. As a good manager, you need an inner strength that will allow you to help an ensemble on the journey, the courage to send other people where you cannot follow, and to let them go. As an ensemble member, you need equal strength and courage, a vocation, to venture into unknown territory, to resist the temptations of the ordinary, to cut yourself free from the comfort of others' opinions, and from the stability of the familiar.

The theatre metaphor offers a clear view into this kind of motivation. In theatre, it's right there, all laid out on top. In keeping with this book's basic premise, we now take a look at the motivations of theatre makers to gain insight into how similar motivations operate in business.

A Last Look at the Theatre

Artful making requires great motive energy to drive past its inherent challenges. In the theatre they call this motive energy *vocation*. The need for it lies in the difficulties of rehearsal and play that we've described, and the complications attendant upon the fact that an actor is both maker and material for the made thing: a character.

Because they are their own material, actors have no way to see and judge the product of their work. The moment they stop working and start watching, the character disappears. You can experience this in the focus exercise we described in Chapter 6: The moment you congratulate yourself on maintaining focus, you've stopped maintaining focus. Characters in movies and television are less clearly, but equally, fleeting. Interventions of editing create such a distance between what happened on the set and what appears on the screen that some actors don't even bother looking at the movies made with their work. For personal satisfaction, they depend on the purity of their methods, on their impeccable process. Actors cannot change the movie—it's out of their hands—but they can work continually to improve their own skills and methods. The good ones do.

An actor makes a character, a product that requires a personal appearance, not only in support of the product (as a sales rep might turn up at the trade show), but *as* the product, presenting his or her very self to the approval or disapproval of paying customers. This vulnerability is a huge obstacle to focus and good work; to overcome it demands great energy. No matter what an actor tells himself, herself, or a friend, that actor *is* the character, just as bricks are the clay of which they're made. If you are an actor, you must take responsibility for being able to do what the character does. There's no way out, no matter how you try.

Because of this hard fact, even good actors sometimes limit their work to familiar categories and routine, avoiding any uncertainty, anything new. In effect, they prove the power of industrial imagery to limit our conception of making:

> I know an actor who works industrially. For him, rehearsal isn't a creation of the script's potential, but a construction of his character out of bits he already knows how to do. He has two main purposes for each rehearsal: (1) to put in his good stuff wherever he can; and (2) to take out anything that doesn't feel comfortable. In the play I saw him rehearse, the resulting character pleased its audience but did not fully exploit the materials of the script. Moreover, the actor's methods interfered amazingly with the others in the cast. Perhaps most importantly, rehearsing (as distinct from accepting applause) never seemed to give him any joy. He was always the one suggesting a break, telling one more story in an interval or discussion, delaying the actual work again and again, as if he didn't really want to do it.[1]

Most actors, even this one, do the work because they can't seem not to. Theatre's a vocation, and those called will do anything to heed the call. In this they're like most other artists.

> It rained on the hay. When the elephants and horses ate the hay, they all got a major case of the trots. The circus train pulled into Brooklyn and the parade to Madison Square Garden began. The clowns who follow with brooms and cans were overworked, to say the least.
>
> At the end of the day, down in the depths of the Garden, two clowns have checked in their brooms and dustpans and are slumped on the bench in front of their lockers, too tired even to shower.
>
> "Man," says one, "was that a day, or what?"
>
> "I'll tell you what," says his partner. "Another day like this and I'm gettin' outta the show business."

Artists (even those who sweep up after the elephants) do their work, not for a paycheck, but because they can't not do it. A look at the pay scale for union actors makes this clear: Those at the very top do strike it rich, but as we're writing this,

most actors earn considerably less than $20K a year doing act-
ing. At any given time, only 10–20% of actors' union members
are actually working as actors; most are filling in with day jobs,
or collecting unemployment and going to auditions. Entry-
level positions in the theatre come with absurdly low wages.
Interns and apprentices routinely *pay* theatres for the opportunity to do grunt work. Could any Fortune 500 company get
young people fresh out of business school to pay for a chance
to sweep up after the elephants?

The point here is that the energy needed to learn and practice artful making in the theatre comes, like the artist's vocation, from an investment in the work that goes beyond a paycheck, into the heart of each individual. Vocation doesn't fully
distinguish between artful and other making, but for artful
making you *must* have it. Artful making is just too hard unless
you want to do it badly enough to take the chances and suffer
the difficulties it demands. Actors and other workers with a
vocation bring this "want to" with them to the party. In more
conventional business environments, we need to look constantly for ways to stimulate this energy.

Vocation means that the work is worth doing for its own
sake. In the terms we've been
using, the results are the work
and the work is the results.
This brings us back to the
interdependency of each quality of artful making with every
other: You cannot separate the dancer from the dance; the
making is the thing made.

> Artful making is just too hard to do unless you want to do it badly enough to take the chances and suffer the difficulties it demands.

To enter this realm, we need to move beyond the popular
notion of a vocation as something assigned to us by an outside
agency. To create a sense of vocation where it doesn't already
exist can be done, but it requires will and imagination. Artists
decide that their work has value. Indeed, this may be the key
feature of artists as a class: they have, by choosing to do their
art, made a further choice to give up the luxury of having
others tell them what their work is worth, how good or bad it
is. They cannot pay attention to reviewers and friends who
presume to judge their performances, because those judges

are not privy to the process. They literally do not know what's going on. They are entitled to their opinions, to their taste about which there's no use arguing, but those opinions have little or no connection to the work artists do. Actors and other artists do their work for the sake of doing their work. While the work is going on, what others think of it is not a central concern.[2]

This sounds like an un-businesslike attitude. It is, and it isn't. It is if your concept of business is dominated by industrial categories, full of plans and goals, efficiency and short-term results. If, on the other hand, your enabling metaphor is drawn from artful rather than industrial making, the artist's view of work is essential.

And liberating.

To discover the joy of working for the sake of doing the work, of work as Play, that's the ultimate purpose, the final cause of artful making. We don't mean work as play in the industrial sense, where that expression is an oxymoron. We mean Play as an essential quality of the kind of work that is its own product, its own reward, but that leads to results that are spectacular, unpredictable, and yes, highly profitable.

Can business people decide to be their own customers? Can they themselves *decide* that their work is a vocation, an end in itself? We believe they can, that many in fact do. If they feel tension between that sense of their work and industrial approaches, the enabling metaphor of artful making can help resolve that. Moreover, this is a way to profit—through innovation and real value creation—a better way than industrial approaches. It's honest work, though, not a way to false value creation, posing, pretending, or accounting flim-flam. It won't work for that.

It's not for everyone, this artful work, and it's not for every application. But members of a working group can, with passionate dedication, release past their edges and inhibitions; they can liberate their creative energies; they can release into a work conversation that generates ideas and actions none of the participants could individually conceive, a conversation that exhibits Collaboration. They can set aside vanity to meet each other on equal terms in their quest for Ensemble, so that their work becomes its own product, their effort its own reward. When they do this, everything changes. The powers of each ensemble member combine in an energy greater than the sum of its parts to create ideas never before conceived.

ENDNOTES

1. Here's the weird part: This actor professed (honestly, I think) to love acting and the theatre (LD).

2. Again we should remark that this is the extreme position, the theoretically most pure and simple. Real life, remarked one of Oscar Wilde's characters, "is rarely pure and never simple." As soon as an artist sells the work, complications ensue and artful making becomes complex, if not impure.

Books

Rafael Aguayo. *Dr. Deming; The American Who Taught the Japanese About Quality*, New York: Carol Publishing Group, 1990.

Christopher Alexander, *The Timeless Way of Building*, New York: Oxford University Press, 1979.

_____. Sara Ishikawa, Murray Silverstein, with Max Jacobson, Ingrid Fiksdahl-King, Shlomo Angel. *A Pattern Language: Towns, Buildings, Construction*, New York: Oxford University Press, 1977.

William F. Allman. *Apprentices of Wonder; Inside the Neural Network Revolution*, New York: Bantam Books, 1989.

*Robert D. Austin. *Measuring and Managing Performance in Organizations*, New York: Dorset House Publishing, 1996.

Patricia Basing. *Trades and Crafts in Medieval Manuscripts*, New York: New Amsterdam Books, 1990.

*Kent Beck. *Extreme Programming Explained; Embrace Change*, Boston: Addison-Wesley, 2000.

Warren Bennis and Patricia Ward Biederman. *Organizing Genius; The Secrets of Creative Collaboration*, Reading MA: Addison Wesley, 1997.

Morris Bishop. *The Middle Ages*, Boston: Houghton Mifflin Company, 1987.

* = cited in the text

Claude Blair, Lionello G. Boccia, Everett Fahy, Helmut Nickel, A. V. B. Norman, Stuart W. Pyhrr and Donald J. La Rocca. *Studies in European Arms and Armor*, The C. Otto von Kienbusch Collection in the Philadelphia Museum of Art, ed. Jane Watkins, Philadelphia: Philadelphia Museum of Art, 1992.

John Briggs and F. David Peat. *Turbulent Mirror: An Illustrated Guide to Chaos Theory and the Science of Wholeness*, New York: Harper & Row, 1989.

Frederick P. Brooks. *The Mythical Man-Month, Anniversary Edition: Essays on Software Engineering*, Boston: Addison-Wesley, 1995.

*Shona L. Brown and Kathleen M. Eisenhardt. *Competing on the Edge: Strategy as Structured Chaos*, Boston: HBS Press, 1998.

*Lewis Carroll. *Alice's Adventures in Wonderland; Through the Looking-Glass*, New York: Collier Books, 1962.

John Cherry. *Medieval Craftsmen: Goldsmiths*, Toronto: University of Toronto Press, 1992.

*Clayton Christensen. *The Innovator's Dilemma*, Boston: HBS Press, 1998.

Marshall Clagett. *The Science of Mechanics in the Middle Ages*, Madison: University of Wisconsin Press, 1959.

*Kim Clark and Takahiro Fujimoto. *Product Development Performance*, Boston: HBS Press, 1991.

*Richard M. Cyert and James G. March. *A Behavioral Theory of the Firm*, Englewood Cliffs NJ: Prentice-Hall, 1963.

Clifford Davidson. *Technology, Guilds, and Early English Drama*, Kalamazoo MI: Medieval Institute Publications, Western Michigan University, Early Drama, Art, and Music Monograph Series, 23, 1996.

Kenneth T. Delavigne and J. Daniel Robertson. *Deming's Profound Changes; When Will the Sleeping Giant Awaken?*, Englewood Cliffs NJ: PTR Prentice Hall, 1994.

*Tom DeMarco and Timothy Lister. *Peopleware; Productive Projects and Teams,* 2nd ed., New York: Dorset House Publishing, 1999.

*W. Edwards Deming. *Out of the Crisis*, Cambridge MA: Massachusetts Institute of Technology, Center for Advanced Engineering Study, 1986.

Albert J. Dunlap, with Bob Andelman. *Mean Business: How I Save Bad Companies and Make Good Companies Great*, New York: Fireside Books, 1997.

Maurice Dumas, ed. *A History of Technology and Invention: Progress Through the Ages*, 2 vols., trans. Eileen B. Hennessy, New York: Crown Publishers, Inc., 1969.

Amy C. Edmondson. "Managing the Risk of Learning: Psychological Safety in Work Teams," in *International Handbook of Organizational Teamwork*, ed. M. West, London: Blackwell, forthcoming.

M. P. Follett. *Creative Experience*, New York: Longmans, Green and Co., 1930.

*_____. *Dynamic Administration; The Collected Papers of Mary Parker Follett*, ed., Henry C. Metcalf and L. Urwick, London: Sir Isaac Pitman & Sons Ltd., [1940].

*Henry Ford. *My Life and Work*. Garden City NY: Doubleday, 1922.

*Paul Freiberger and Michael Swaine. *Fire in the Valley: The Making of the Personal Computer*, Collector's Edition, Boston: McGraw-Hill, 1999.

Andrea Gabor. *The Man Who Discovered Quality*, New York: Random House, Times Books, 1990.

*William Gibson. *The Seesaw Log*, New York: Alfred A. Knopf, 1959.

James Gleick. *Chaos; Making a New Science*, New York: Viking, 1987.

Constance McL. Green. *Eli Whitney and the Birth of American Technology*, ed., Oscar Handlin, Boston and Toronto: Little, Brown and Company, 1956.

*Alec Guinness. *Blessings in Disguise*, New York: Alfred A. Knopf, 1986.

*Gary Hamel. *Leading the Revolution*, Boston: HBS Press, 2000.

W. O. Hassall, ed. *Medieval England, As Viewed by Contemporaries*, Harper Torchbooks, New York: Harper & Row, 1965.

*James A. Highsmith III. *Adaptive Software Development: A Collaborative Approach to Managing Complex Systems*, New York: Dorset House Publishing, 2000.

*_____. *Agile Software Developoment: Principles, Practices, and Ecosystems*, Boston: Addison-Wesley, 2002.

*Michael A. Hiltzik. *Dealers of Lightning: Xerox PARC and the Dawn of the Computer Age*, New York: Harper Collins, 1999.

Erich Jantsch. *Design for Evolution: Self-Organization and Planning in the Life of Human Systems*, New York: G. Braziller, 1975.

_____. *The Self-Organizing Universe: Scientific and Human Implications of the Emerging Paradigm of Evolution*, New York: G. Braziller, 1980.

_____ and Conrad H. Waddington, eds. *Evolution and Consciousness: Human Systems in Transition*, Reading MA: Addison-Wesley, 1976.

*Robert Kanigel. *The One Best Way: Frederick Winslow Taylor and the Enigma of Efficiency*, New York: Viking, 1997.

*Tom Kelly, with Jonathan Littman. *The Art of Innovation; Lessons in Creativity from IDEO, America's Leading Design Firm*, A Currency Book, New York: Doubleday, 2001.

John Kobler. *Damned in Paradise:The Life of John Barrymore*, New York: Atheneum, 1975.

*Gene Kranz. *Failure is Not an Option: Mission Control from Mercury to Apollo 13 and Beyond*, New York: Simon and Schuster, 2000.

Brenda Laurel. *Computers as Theatre*, Reading MA: Addison-Wesley Publishing Company, 1991.

Art Linson. *A Pound of Flesh; Producing Movies in Hollywood—Perilous Tales from the Trenches*, New York: Avon Books, 1993.

*Dorothy A. Leonard-Barton. *Wellsprings of Knowledge: Building and Sustaining the Sources of Innovation*, Boston: HBS Press, 1995.

*Dorothy Leonard and Walter Swap. *When Sparks Fly: Igniting Creativity in Groups*, Boston: HBS Press, 1999.

Jacques Le Goff. *Medieval Civilization, 400–1500*, trans., Julia Barrow, London: Basil Blackwell Ltd., 1988.

Alan M. MacEachren. *How Maps Work: Representation, Visualization, and Design*, New York: The Guilford Press, 1995.

John A. Mills. *Hamlet on Stage; The Great Tradition*. Westport CT: Greenwood Press, 1985.

*Jeannette Mirsky and Allan Nevins. *The World of Eli Whitney*, New York: The Macmillan Company, 1952.

*Edward Miller and John Hatcher. *Medieval England; Rural Society and Economic Change, 1086–1348*, London: Longman, 1978.

Mark Monmonier. *How to Lie with Maps*, 2nd ed., Chicago: The University of Chicago Press, 1996.

William Morris, ed. *The American Heritage Dictionary of the English Language*, New College Edition, Boston: Houghton Mifflin Company, 1979.

*Allan Nevins. *Ford: The Times, the Man, the Company*, with the collaboration of Frank Ernest Hill, New York: Charles Scribner's Sons, 1954.

George Ovitt, Jr. *The Restoration of Perfection; Labor and Technology in Medieval Culture*. New Brunswick NJ: Rutgers University Press, 1986.

Matthias Pfaffenbichler. *Medieval Craftsmen: Armourers*, Toronto: University of Toronto Press, 1992.

*B. Joseph Pine, James H. Gilmore, and B. Joseph Pine II. *The Experience Economy*, Boston: HBS Press, 1999.

Norman John Greville Pounds. *An Economic History of Medieval Europe*, London, New York: Longman, 1974.

*James Brian Quinn. *Strategies for Change; Logical Incrementalism*, Homewood IL: Irwin, 1980.

Eric S. Raymond. *The Cathedral & the Bazaar; Musings on Linux and Open Source by an Accidental Revolutionary*, Cambridge MA: O'Reilly, 1999.

*Michael Schrage. *Serious Play: How the World's Best Companies Simulate to Innovate*, Boston: HBS Press, 2000.

*Joseph A. Schumpeter. *Capitalism, Socialism, and Democracy*, New York: Harper, 1975.

*William Shakespeare. *Hamlet*, ed. Harold Jenkins, *The Arden Edition of the Works of William Shakespeare*, gen. ed. Richard Proudfoot, London and New York: Metheun, 1982.

*Frederick Winslow Taylor. *The Principles of Scientific Management*, New York: W. W. Norton, 1957.

Jerome Taylor. Translation from the Latin with an introduction and notes, *The* Didascalicon *of Hugh of St. Victor; a Medieval Guide to the Arts*, New York: Columbia University Press, 1961.

Kenneth A. Telford. *Aristotle's* Poetics, *Translation and Analysis*, Lanham MD: University Press of America, 1985.

*Lewis Thomas. *The Youngest Science; Notes of a Medicine-Watcher*, New York: The Viking Press, 1983.

Albert Payson Usher. *A History of Mechanical Inventions*, rev. ed., Cambridge MA: Harvard University Press, 1962.

Peter B. Vaill. *Managing as a Performing Art: New Ideas for a World of Chaotic Change*, San Francisco and London: Jossey-Bass Inc., 1989.

Frank T. Vertosick, Jr. *The Genius Within; Discovering the Intelligence of Every Living Thing*, New York: Harcourt, 2002.

Mary Walton. *Deming Management at Work*, New York: G. P. Putnam's Sons, 1990.

Karl E. Weick. *The Social Psychology of Organizing*, Reading MA: Addison-Wesley, 1979.

T. D. Weldon. *The Vocabulary of Politics*, London: Penguin Books, 1953.

Margaret J. Wheatley. *Leadership and the New Science; Learning about Organization from an Orderly Universe*, San Francisco: Berret-Koehler Publishers, Inc., 1994.

Lynn White, Jr. *Medieval Technology and Social Change*, London: Oxford University Press, 1962.

Elspeth Whitney. *Paradise Restored: the Mechanical Arts from Antiquity through the Thirteenth Century*, Transactions of the American Philosophical Society, vol. 80, Part 1, 1990, Philadelphia: The American Philosophical Society, 1990.

*Toby Silverman Zinman, ed. *Terrence McNally, A Casebook*, New York: Garland Publishing Group, Inc., 1997.

PERIODICALS

*Anonymous. *Cycle and Automobile Trade Journal*, X (January 1, 1906).

*Robert D. Austin and Partick D. Larkey. "Performance Based Incentives in Knowledge Work: Are Agency Models Relevant?," *International Journal of Business Performance Management*, 2, no. 1/2/3 (2000), 57.

*Barry Boehm. "A Spiral Model of Software Development and Enhancement," *IEEE Computer*, 21, no. 5 (May 1988), 61.

H. Kent Bowen and Steven Spear. "Decoding the DNA of the Toyota Production System," *Harvard Business Review*, September 1999, 96.

Amy Edmondson. "Psychological Safety and Learning Behavior in Work Teams," *Administrative Science Quarterly*, 44, no. 4 (1999), 350.

*Amy Edmondson, Richard Bohmer, and Gary P. Pisano. "Disrupted Routines: Team Learning and New Technology Adaptation," *Administrative Science Quarterly*, 46, (2001), 685.

*Malcolm Gladwell, "The Talent Myth," *The New Yorker*, 22 July 2002, 26.

*Frederick P. Brooks, Jr. "No Silver Bullet: Essence and Accidents of Software Engineering," *IEEE Computer*, 20, no. 4 (April 1987), 10-19.

*Kathleen M. Eisenhardt. "Making Fast Strategic Decisions in High-Velocity Environments," *Academy of Management Journal*, 32, no. 3 (1989), 543.

*Kathleen M. Eisenhardt and Benham N. Tabrizi. "Accelerating Adaptive Processes: Product Innovation in the Global Computer Industry," *Administrative Science Quarterly*, 40, no. 1 (1995), 84-110.

*J. C. R. Licklider. "Man-Computer Symbiosis," *IRE Transactions on Human Factors in Electronics*, HFE-1 (March 1960), 4-11.

*Alan D. MacCormack and Marco Iansiti. "Developing Products on Internet Time," *Harvard Business Review*, September-October 1997, 108.

*Henry Mintzberg and Alexandra McHugh. "Strategy Formation in an Adhocracy," *Administrative Science Quarterly*, 30, no. 2 (June 1985), 160-197.

*Richard T. Pascale. "Perspectives on Strategy: The Real Story Behind Honda's Success," *California Management Review*, 26, no. 3 (1984), 47-72.

*William A. Sahlman. "How to Write a Great Business Plan," *Harvard Business Review*, July-August 1997, 98.

*Richard Sandomir. "Lots of Waggles to See, but Little Suspense," *New York Times*, 17 June 2002, D4.

*Stefan H. Thomke. "Enlightened Experimentation: The New Imperative for Innovation," *Harvard Business Review*, February 2001, 67.

CASES AND WORKING PAPERS

*Teresa M. Amabile, et al. "Time Pressure and Creativity in Organizations: A Longitudinal Field Study," HBS Working Paper 02-073, 2002.

*Robert D. Austin. "The People's Light and Theatre Company," HBS case no. 600-055, 2000.

*_____. "Trilogy (A)," HBS case no. 699-034, 1999.

*_____. "Trilogy (B)," HBS case no. 600-123, 2000.

*_____ and Mark J. Cotteleer. "Ford Motor Company: Maximizing the Business Value of Web Technologies," HBS case no. 198-006, 1998.

*_____ and Richard L. Nolan. "Manage ERP Initiatives as New Ventures, Not IT Projects," HBS Working Paper no. 99-024, 1998.

*_____, Richard L. Nolan, and Mark J. Cotteleer. "Cisco Systems, Inc.: Implementing ERP," HBS case no. 699-022, 1999.

*_____, Richard L. Nolan, Mark J. Cotteleer, and George Westerman. "Tektronix, Inc.: Global ERP Implementation," HBS case no. 699-043, 1999.

*Carliss Baldwin and Kim Clark. "The Value and Consequences of Modularity in Design: A Summary of the Argument," in *Design Rules* 1, HBS Working Paper, 14 March 2002.

*Mark Cotteleer and Robert D. Austin. "Sun Microsystems: Realizing the Business Value of Web Technologies" HBS case no. 198-007, 1998.

*David A. Garvin and Janet Simpson. "Digital Equipment Corp.: The Endpoint Model (A)," HBS case no. 688-059, 1988.

*_____. "Digital Equipment Corp.: The Endpoint Model (B1), HBS case no. 688-060, 1988.

*_____. "Digital Equipment Corp.: The Endpoint Model (B2), HBS case no. 688-061, 1988.

*_____. "Digital Equipment Corp.: The Endpoint Model (C1), HBS case no. 688-062, 1988.

*_____. "Digital Equipment Corp.: The Endpoint Model (C2), HBS case no. 688-063, 1988.

*Marc Mandel and Robert D. Austin. "Trilogy (C)," HBS case no. 601-140, 2001.

*Gary P. Pisano. "BMW: The 7-Series Project (A)," HBS case no. 692-083, 1993.

*Nicole Tempest and F. Warren McFarlan. "Charles Schwab Corporation (A)," HBS case no. 300-024, 1999.

*_____. "Charles Schwab Corporation (B)," HBS case no. 300-025, 1999.

*Stefan Thomke and Ashok Nimgade. "IDEO Product Development," HBS case no. 600-143, 2000.

*David M. Upton. "The Cybertech Project (A)," HBS case no. 695-030, 1995.

*_____ and Sari Carp. "HMS Thetis and Apollo XIII," HBS case no. 696-097, 1996.

*_____ and Joshua Margolis. "McDonald's Corporation," HBS case no. 693-028, 1992.

VIDEO

Apollo 13: To the Edge and Back, dir. Noel Buckner and Rob Whittlesey, WGBH Public Television, 1994.

We owe thanks to a large number of people who contributed, in one way or another, to the creation of this book. We are grateful to Dean Kim Clark and the Division of Research at the Harvard Business School, who funded much of the research involved in this project. Similarly, we are indebted to Swarthmore College and its president, Al Bloom, for support of Lee's work on the project, especially for a leave provided during the writing; we owe Swarthmore gratitude as well for maintaining the rich intellectual environment that planted the seeds of this project almost 20 years ago, when Rob was a student in Lee's classroom.

We offer thanks to many friends and colleagues who read our manuscript, some of them in more than one version, and provided feedback and encouragement, or who reacted to our ideas in seminars or one-on-one. These include, at Harvard Business School: Jonathan West (who collaborated in our early research), Clay Christensen, Bob Hayes, Dorothy Leonard, Warren McFarlan, Dick Nolan, Gary Pisano, Roy Shapiro, and Stefan Thomke; and at Swarthmore College: Charles Gilbert and David Smith. In industry, Lucinda Duncalfe Holt, Joe Liemandt, Barbara Moss, Skip Shuda, and others in many companies who gave generously of their time and ideas. Karen Coburn and other members of the Cutter Consortium, including IT industry luminaries such as Kent Beck, Alastair Cockburn, Christine Davis, Tom DeMarco, Jim Highsmith, Tim Lister, Ken Orr, and Ed Yourdon also provided encouragement and useful inputs, as well as expert opinions about the agile software movement.

Lee extends a special thanks to friends and colleagues who read, talked, and told stories "too numerous to mention": Doris

Baizley, Brian Doerner, Kathleen Devin, Sean Devin, Lue Douthit, Mitchell Eil, Kent Emery, Christine Fredericks, Lynn Thomson, Joy Mills, David Mooberry, Geoff Proehl, Mark Schwartz, Philip Tankel, Gordon Wickstrom, Michele Volansky, and David Weiss stand out among many.

Many people helped us during the course of research and manuscript preparation. Donna Kennedy's extraordinary generosity made our first draft possible. Research Assistants Alastair Brown, Michael Cruz, Joe Gúzman, Amanda Hatch, Marc Mandel, Steve Salter, and Erin Sullivan conducted interviews, performed analyses, and chased logistical details throughout our work in the field. Faculty assistants Brooke Spangler and Zoya Omartian contributed their thorough and conscientious work, as well as substantive suggestions.

Our editors at Financial Times Prentice Hall, Tim Moore, Russ Hall, and Wil Mara, have provided expert guidance as we worked our way through the development and production of the manuscript; many thanks to each of them. We also owe a debt to several anonymous reviewers, whose feedback helped us mold the book into its current form. We owe a huge debt as well to a reviewer who was not anonymous—Tom DeMarco—who provided the most thorough and helpful review either of us has ever encountered. No thanks can be adequate for the good he did us at a crucial time in the development of the manuscript.

We both offer a special thanks to the People's Light and Theatre Company, and to all of its staff and artists, who allowed us to invade their rehearsals and to observe them at work in ways that are not at all customary. Their willingness to be examined closely was an important part of the making of this book and remains vital to our ongoing research project.

With Laurel Austin and Abigail Adams, we, of course, carry long-standing deficit accounts. No thanks will ever be adequate to settle those. Thanks also to all of the members of our families, for their support and patience.

Rob Austin
Westborough, MA

Lee Devin
Swarthmore, PA

A

8 reasons why you should read the Financial Times for 4 weeks RISK-FREE!

To help you stay current with significant
developments in the world economy ...
and to assist you to make informed business
decisions — the Financial Times brings you:

1 Fast, meaningful overviews of international affairs ... plus daily
briefings on major world news.

2 Perceptive coverage of economic, business, financial and political
developments with special focus on emerging markets.

3 More international business news than any other publication.

4 Sophisticated financial analysis and commentary on world market
activity plus stock quotes from over 30 countries.

5 Reports on international companies and a section on global investing.

6 Specialized pages on management, marketing, advertising and
technological innovations from all parts of the world.

7 Highly valued single-topic special reports (over 200 annually)
on countries, industries, investment opportunities, technology and more.

8 The Saturday Weekend FT section — a globetrotter's guide to
leisure-time activities around the world: the arts, fine dining, travel,
sports and more.

FT FINANCIAL TIMES
World business newspaper

The *Financial Times* delivers a world of business news.

Use the Risk-Free Trial Voucher below!

To stay ahead in today's business world you need to be well-informed on a daily basis. And not just on the national level. You need a news source that closely monitors the entire world of business, and then delivers it in a concise, quick-read format.

With the *Financial Times* you get the major stories from every region of the world. Reports found nowhere else. You get business, management, politics, economics, technology and more.

Now you can try the *Financial Times* for 4 weeks, absolutely risk free. And better yet, if you wish to continue receiving the *Financial Times* you'll get great savings off the regular subscription rate. Just use the voucher below.

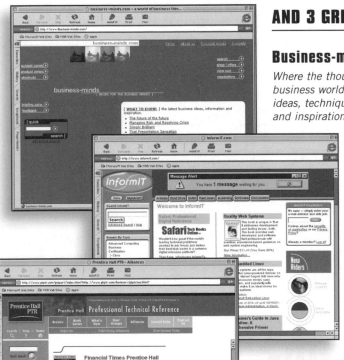